Social Philosophy of Swami Vivekananda

"He who has served and helped one poor man seeing Shiva in him, without thinking of his caste, or creed, or race, or anything, with him Shiva is more pleased than with the man who sess Him only in the temples."

Swami Vivekananda

About the Author

Dr. Amulya Ranjan Mohapatra at present is Director of Swami Vivekananda Swadhyay Kendra, President of Swami Vivekananda Banabharati Vidyapith, and Secretary of Sri Ramakrishna Sat-Sangha, Koraput (Orissa). He taught Logic and Philosophy at various Government Colleges and also worked as Vice-Principal and Principal before his retirement. He has contributed numerous articles to several newspapers and journals of repute.

Dr. Mohapatra has to his credit many books including The Idea of Inexpressible: A Philosophical Analysis, Philosophy of Religion, Hinduism: Analytical Study, Value System, Indian Freedom Fighter, Bir Surendra Sai, Bharatiya Dharma O Darsana, Sri Ramakrishna Jivana Darsana, Swaraj: A Multi-Dimensional Concept.

Social Philosophy
of
Swami Vivekananda

Dr. A.R. Mohapatra

Readworthy
New Delhi

Disclaimer from the author: All religions/beliefs and schools of philosophy are equally respected and statement of any kind does not endorse or prefer one over the other. The beliefs, thoughts, convictions, suitability, benefits, etc. expressed are all personal to me. Any narration, belief, indication, conclusion, method or similar statement should not be construed as recommendations. Those may and would not suit to all or even anybody in some case. These are not to be taken as a panacea. Nothing is promised. The reader may or may not follow what is stated; he or she may do so only by using his or her own personal discretion and at his or her own responsibility.

First published 2009

Readworthy Publications (P) Ltd.

Regd. Off
A-18, Mohan Garden
Near Nawada Metro Station
New Delhi – 110 059 (India)
Phone: 011-2537 1324
Fax: +91-11-2537 1323

Branch
4735/22, Prakash Deep Building,
Ground Floor, Ansari Road, Daryaganj
New Delhi – 110 002
Phone: 011-43549197
Fax: +91-11-23243060

Email: info@readworthypub.com Web: www.readworthypub.com

Cataloging in Publication Data–DK

Courtesy: D.K. Agencies (P) Ltd. <docinfo@dkagencies.com>

Mohapatra, Amulya Ranjan.

Social philosophy of Swami Vivekananda / A.R. Mohapatra.

p. cm.

Swami Vivekananda, 1863-1902, Indian philosopher and religious leader.

Includes bibliographical references.

Includes index.

ISBN 13: 978-93-80009-00-1 ISBN 10: 93-80009-00-3

1. Vivekananda, Swami, 1863-1902. 2. Social sciences--Philosophy. I. Title.

DDC 300.1 22

Printed at Salasar Imaging Systems, Delhi - 35

This work is dedicated to
Swami Vivekananda
with regards and devotion.

Preface

At present the modern man is a victim of various conflicting forces which stand in the way of his self-realisation. But one should not feel despair and disappointment as a dynamic philosopher Swami Vivekananda's life and social philosophy are always there to save as a source of great inspiration to all of us. His eternal words give courage to a depressed mind and his optimistic message provide hope for a sinking nation.

Swami Vivekananda had said, 'A hundred thousand men and women, fired with the zeal of holiness, fortified with eternal faith in the Lord, and nerved to lion's courage by their sympathy for the poor and the fallen and the downtrodden, will go over the length and breath of the land, preaching the gospel of salvation, the gospel of help, the gospel of social raising-up—the gospel of equality."

This study is mainly intended to meet the needs of those who, with all their earnestness, want to serve the motherland wholeheartedly in the form of worshipping her as a living God.' Out of many sided activities of Swami Vivekananda. In this study an attempt has been made to take a look at the social philosophy of Swami Vivekananda..

In preparing this U.G.C. research project I am highly grateful to the authorities of University Grants

Commission, Calcutta office, for having awarded me this financial research grant to complete this noble work.

I am thankful to my wife Mrs. Bijaya Mohaptra, two daughters, Mama and Papa for their co-operation and inspiration. I am also heavily indebted to my institution, D.A.V. College, Koraput, Orissa that has assisted me in various ways to do this work. Today it came to the form of a book by the Readworthy Publisher, New Delhi to whom I convey my Sincere thanks and gratitude.

Jan. 12. 2009

Amulya Ranjan Mohapatra

Contents

1

Introduction

Swami Vivekananda was a multi-faceted personality—a great spiritual teacher who ceaselessly worked for the good of all humanities. Whatever he said or did was not only for the salvation of India but for the removal of misery from the world, and above all his goal was help all human beings could attain the knowledge of their divine nature. His message was, therefore, not for one time, but for all times-not for one country, but for all countries, not for one aspect of human life but for all aspects of human existence.

Swami Vivekananda was a great monk who dedicated his life to the welfare of the masses. He used his energies for the betterment of man everywhere, materially and morally. He was well aware of the pitiable condition of the poor masses of the country and his heart bled at what he saw. His love for India was the product of his love for man. To awaken men and women everywhere to their divine birthright was his life's mission. It was indeed a rare mission of a monk who had devoted his life for the upliftment of the masses. He realised that service to mankind equalled service to God. If service is rendered in the true spirit of worship, it is the most efficacious means to spiritual realisation, for man is the highest symbol of God and the service to man is the highest form of worship on earth.

Swami Vivekananda said he was a socialist, adding at the same time, 'not that socialism is perfect, but half a loaf is better than none.' He was a socialist so far as he believed that adequate opportunities of growth should be given to all.

In the modern age, Swami Vivekananda gifted India with two of her crying needs, namely, national consciousness and socialism. "His contribution to the awakening of India raised him," in the opinion of Lokamanya Bal Gangadhar Tilak, "to the status of Shankaracharya." Every great national leader, subsequent to Swami Vivekananda, has acknowledged having received inspiration from him. In the Swadeshi agitation, Sri Aurobindo remarked that Vivekananda was a soul of puissance if ever there was one, a very lion among men; and to Netaji Subhash Chandra Bose, Swami Vivekananda was be regarded as the spiritual father of the modern Nationalist Movement. Mahatma Gandhi proclaimed that by studying the works of Vivekananda, his love for his motherland increased a hundredfold, and his movement for the upliftment of the scheduled caste had behind it, the tremendous inspiration of Vivakananda's powerful crusade against casteism and untouchability. According to Rabindranath Tagore, "Swamiji inspired the daring deeds of the youth and awakened in them the spirit of dedication and service to the nation."[1]

Vivekananda's socialism was not merely a product of an emotional upsurage of human compassion. It was based on a social philosophy of man and his infinite possibilities—the philosophy of *Advaita*, which proclaims the divinity and solidarity of all human beings. He, thus, connected the modern political and social democratic for freedom and equality with India's ancient *Vedantic* philosophy.

In the light of this spirituality, he opposed the concept groups or section of the society. He was the first spiritual teacher in history who dealt with socio-economic problems of man, along with his religious cravings and aspiration. He could do so because the philosophy of *Advaita*, which he and his teacher Sri Ramakrishna upheld, is a unifying philosophy oriented to action in the world.

Swami Vivekananda was impressed by the material prosperity of the West, but he had also observed how it had blunted its moral perceptions. He wanted India to attain the same material prosperity yet retain her love for moral

---

1 My India, The India Eternal, Swami Vivekananda The Ramakrishna Mission Institute of Cuttune, Calcutta, 1997, page.195-196.

values. Morality, of course, is not the goal of man, but the means through which freedom is attained. "That action is moral," according to him, "which frees us from the bondage of matter and vice versa."[2]

Everything that we perceive around us is struggling towards freedom, from an atom to man, from the insentient lifeless particle of matter to the highest existence on earth, the human soul. The whole universe is, in fact, the result of this struggle for freedom. There is to be found in every religion the manifestation of this struggle towards freedom, it is the groundwork of all morality. When we see a man doing good work, helping others, it means that he cannot be confined within the limited circle of me and mine. 'All the great systems of ethics preach absolute unselfishness as the goal. *Karma yoga* is attaining through unselfish work, of that freedom which is the goal of all human nature. Every action must be done as duty, only for the sake of doing work, without thinking of its result; to Swami Vivekananda that which is selfish is immoral, and that which is unselfish is moral.'[3]

The watchword of all well-being, of all moral good is not 'I' but 'thou.' Who cares whether there is a heaven or a hell, who cares if there is a soul or not? Here is the world and it is full of misery. Go out into it, as Buddha did, and struggle

---

2 Complete Works of Swami Vivekananda, Vol-VII p. 102.

3 Ibid-Vol-Ipp.108-10.

to lessen it.' Swami Vivekananda said that 'forget yourselves whether you are a theist or an atheist, whether you are an agnostic or a Vedantist, a Christian or a Mohammedan. The one lesson obvious to all is the destruction of the little self and the building up of the real self.[4]

"Spiritual knowledge is the only thing that can destroy our miseries for ever; any other knowledge satisfies wants only for a short time. He who gives man spiritual knowledge is the greatest benefactor of mankind and as such we always find that those were the most powerful of men who helped man in his spiritual needs, because spirituality is the true basis of all our activities in life."[5]

Helping others physically, by removing their physical needs, is indeed, great, but the help is greater as the need is greater and according as the help is far reaching........The help which tends to make us strong spiritually is the highest, next to it comes intellectual help, and after that physical help. The miseries of the world cannot be cured by physical help only. Until man's nature changes, these physical needs will always arise, and the miseries will always be felt and no amount of physical help will cure

---

4 C.W.VII P353

5 C.W.V.I.P 52

them completely. The only solution of this problem is to make mankind pure.[6]

Swami Vivekananda's interpretation of religion was *Vedantic* unity practiced through service based on equality and renunciation (*Tyaga*). He brought men, societies and religions nearer to God. Service as a pathway to God became Swami Vivekananda's great contribution to religion. In the process, religion became more relevant to people, who saw equality through service as applied and spiritualised socialism, a socialism without a class-war or conflict.

The national ideals of India are renunciation and service. Swami Vivekananda said "None lives except he who lives for others, the rest are more dead than alive."[7] However, by 'service' Swami Vivekananda did not mean mere charity, admirable as this might be.

From his teacher, Sri Ramkrishna, Swami Vivekananda learnt the invaluable gospel of Shiva Jhane Jive Seva which meant sieving every being as the manifestation of God. Vivekananda analysed this doctrine as the gist of all worships—....to be pure and to do good to others. He who sees Shiva in the poor, in the weak, and in the diseased, really worships Shiva to be and if he sees shiva only in the image, his worship is but preliminary. He

---

6 C.W.V.I.P 52, 53.

7 Letters of Swami Vivekananda-III.

who has served and helped one poor man seeing Shiva in him, without thinking of his caste, or creed, or race, or anything, with him Shiva is more pleased than with the man who sees him only in temples'.

Swami Vivekananda asked us to follow our national ideals of renunciation and service. Without renunciation none can pour out his whole heart in working for others. Service for the welfare of the people should be the motto of mankind. Concern for the well-being of humanity, all over the world, remained the primal driving force for him. He affirmed his attitude, thus 'I am the worshipper of *Daridranarayana,* of the Narayana who is located in all the poor people of the world. It is my duty to look after them all. The best way to reach God is by the service of man.'

It is significant that in the practical application of his Master's grand ideal of service, Swami Vivekananda offered a synthetic ideal by juxtaposing the vow of service to humanity with the classical vow of one's own liberation. He coined the phrase *'Atmano moksartham_ jagaddhitaya ca'* as the motto of the Ramakrishna Movement. It means one should aspire for the liberation of the soul and for the good of the world.

Swami Vivekananda said that "you cannot help anyone, you can only serve the children of the Lord, serve the Lord Himself, if you have the privilege. Do it only as worship.' He also said that the poor, the downtrodden, the ignorant let those be your God. God is present in every Jiva"[8] Swamiji was for the uplift of everybody, every where. He was positive, not negative.

When our country today is passing through the momentous revolutionary transition, the inspiring and the humanistic social philosophy of Swami Vivekananda will help our people achieve alround upliftment, giving them a new vision of life.

---

8 C.W.V.III P. 246.

2

Social Life of Swami Vivekananda

"A hundred thousand men and women, fired with the zeal of holiness, fortified with eternal faith in the Lord, and nerved lion's courage by their sympathy for the poor and the fallen and the downtrodden, will go over the length and breadth of the land, preaching the gospel of salvation, the gospel of help, the gospel of social raising-up, the gospel of equality" (V 15) (The complete works of Swami Vivekananda.)

It shows the attitude and the intention of Swami Vivekananda as per his social life is concerned. It would be more clear and vivid if some of the memorable events of his life were reproduced here.

Some people are born with kind and loving hearts. They always try to help other people. Swami Vivekananda was like that even during his childhood days.

Many saints and beggars came to his house almost everyday for food or money. 'Narendranath or Naren, as Vivekananda was then known, used to offer...' anything that was handy. He never thought how much it might cost his father! He would give away even the most costly things.

One day Naren was locked by his mother in a room upstairs to teach him a good lesson. Soon he heard a beggar calling out. Naren wanted to give the poor man something. He looked around the room. He found one trunk that was not locked. Quickly, Naren opened it and took out some saris. He opened a window and saw a beggar standing just below the window. He was dressed in rags. His body was nothing but bones. Naren felt very sorry for him and threw down the saris to the man. The poor beggar was very pleased at this kindness of the little boy.

Narendra's father, Vishwanath Datta, was well known for his charity. Vishwanath was a benevolent person. He used to help the needy and poor people of the society. Narendranath was very much influenced by his father and from his childhood days he was very generous and kind to all. He found a complete expression of this sympathy in the life and teachings of Sri Ramakrishna who transformed his natural compassion into love and reverence for everyone and everything. Shri Ramakrishna taught him that pity is not enough. The right kind of attitude, according to Shri Ramakrishna, should be to serve *Jiva* as *Shiva*, to serve humanity as the manifestation of Divinity.

Swami Vivekananda learnt from his Master to treat every man, even the fallen one, with respect. He used to say' God the wicked,' 'God the sinner.' If in this hell of a world one can bring a little joy and peace even for a day into the heart of a single person, that much alone is true; this I have learnt after suffering all my life.'

Once someone told Vivekananda that the monk should have no particular attachment to his country. Instead, he should view all countries as his own. At this, swamiji replied: "He who fails to love and support his mother how can he provide sustenance for another mother?" What he meant was that even the *sannyasins* should love their motherland'. How can he who cannot love his own country, embrace the world? Patriotism first, then universalism.

He often used to tell his disciples that he who does not try to do good to others can hardly be called a *Sannyasin*. He repeatedly said that a *Sannyasin* is born to live for others. He is there to redress the worldly sufferings of mortals as well as to take care of their spiritual need.

An interesting incident took place when Swami Vivekananda was living the life of a wandering monk. Sometimes he spent the night at a burning *ghat*, sometimes he used to sleeps in the palace of a king, sometimes he took rest at a railway station but he was always happy. Once while he was resting at a railway station in Rajasthan, people kept coming to him all day long. They had many questions mostly religious, and he tirelessly answered them. Three days and three nights passed in this manner. He was so engrossed in talking about spiritual matters that he did not even stop to eat.

The people who flocked him to also did not think of asking him if he had any food to eat.

On the third night of his stay there, when the visitors had all left, a poor man came forward and said to him lovingly, 'Swamiji, I have noticed that for three days you have been talking and talking. You have not taken even a drop of water. This has pained me very much.' Vivekananda felt that God had appeared before him in the form of a poor man. He looked at him and said, "Will you please give me something to eat?" The man was a cobbler by profession, so he said with some hesitation, 'Swamiji, my heart yearns to give you some bread, but how can I? I have touched it. If you permit, I will bring you some coarse flour and dal and you can prepare them as you please!'

Vivekananda said, 'No, my child, give me the bread you have baked. I shall be happy to eat it.' The poor man was frightened at first. He feared the King might punish him if he came to know that he, a low caste person, had prepared food for a *Sannyasin*. But the eagerness to serve a monk overpowered his fear. He hurriedly went back home and soon returned with freshly baked bread. The kindness and unselfish love of this penurious man brought tears to Vivekananda's eyes. How many persons like this live in the huts of our country unnoticed, he thought. They are materially poor and of so-called humble origin, yet they are so noble and large hearted.

In the meantime, some gentlemen found out that Vivekananda was eating food offered by a shoemaker and were very annoyed. They went to him and told him that it was improper for him to accept food from a man of low birth; Vivekananda patiently heard them and than said, "You people made me talk without respite for the last three days, but you did not even care to inquire me whether I had taken any food and rest. You claim you are gentlemen and boast of your high caste. What is more shameful, you condemn this man for being of a low caste. Can you overlook the humanity he has just shown and despise him without feeling ashamed?'

One winter Swami Vivekananda went to Deoghar as a guest of a devotee. One day while taking a walk with his brother-disciple, he saw a helpless man lying by the side of the road writhing in pain. He moved closer to the man and found he was suffering from acute dysentery. Reading the man needed, medical treatment, he brought the man to a house and cleaned him thoroughly, clothed him and applied hot formentations. As a result, the unknown patient soon recovered. This was the kind of service rendered unhesitately by Vivekananda towards a man.

On another occasion when Vivekananda was travelling by train, a poor Muslim hawker selling boiled gram boarded his compartment. As soon as he saw the hawker, he started speaking with the *Brahmachari* accompanying him about the benefits of eating gram. The *Brahmachari* understood Vivekananda's motive and brought gram worth one paise but paid the man four annas.

Vivekananda asked the *Brahmachari* how much he had paid. 'Four annas,' replied the *Brahmachari*. At this Vivekananda said to him affectionately, 'My child that is too little! He has a wife and children at home. Give him a rupee.'

Swami Vivekananda first lecture at Parliament of Religions in Chicago made him very famous and many distinguished people of Chicago invited him home as their guest. He was given a royal reception by scholars and intellectuals. However, he neither hankered after name and fame nor did he want physical comfort. He could not forget how much his countrymen were suffeing. His heart continued to bleed for India and he could not sleep on the luxurious bed. He lay on the floor and wept like a child the whole night. He prayed; 'O Mother, who cares for fame wnen my country is bogged down in deep poverty! Who will raise the Indians and give them food? O Mother, tell me how I can serve them.'

A similar incident took place during his stay at Belur *Math* his. 'Swami Vijnananda, a brother disciple was woken one night by the sounds of sobbing. Realising that the sounds came from Vivekananda's room he rushed to him and inquired after his health. Vivekananda replied."....' "No my dear, I am not sick . But I cannot sleep as long as my country suffers. I was crying and praying to Shri Ramakrishna that we would soon see better days.'

Vivekananda was not in the best of his health since his return from the, West. His health was deteriorating day by day. Heading to the advice of his brother monks, disciples and well wishers, he headed towards Darjeeiing for a change.

One day, during his morning walk, Vivekananda saw a poor Bhutia woman treading along with a heavy load on her back. Suddenly she stumbled and fell down with the entire load. She sustained serious injuires on herbs. Vivekananda was pained to see her plight and could feel the same excruciating pain within himself."

Although famous and worshipped by thousands of devotees both at home and abroad Vivekananda remained the same old 'Naren' to them throughout.

When in Lahore, he once met his boyhood friend Motilal Bose, who owned the Great Indian Circus. Having met his friend after a long time Vivekananda plunged into conversation with him. Motilal however, felt uneasy. He said 'Brother, how should I address you, as 'Naren' or 'Swamiji?'

Vivekananda burst out laughing and said; Are you crazy? My dear Moti, nothing has changed. You are to me the same 'Moti' and I am 'Naren.' Swami ji uttered these words with so much love and tenderness that.

Many rich people, who were devoted to Swami Vivekananda, invited him to dinner during his brief stay at Alwar, but he first chose to visit a poor old woman, who during his wandering days, had offered him food when he had nothing to eat. On reaching Alwar, he sent her a message asking to be treated with some of the same thick chapatis he was offered years before which he relished very much.

The old woman was beside herself with joy. She prepared the chapatis with great care and waited upon the Swami and his disciples eagerly. When they came, she lovingly served them the simple meal, lived by all. Before parting Vivekananda silently thrust a hundred rupee note into the hands of the master of the house to be given to the old woman.

A north Indian pundit once visited Vivekananda with the intention of outshining him in a discussion on *Vedanta*, but Vivekananda was then not in a mood to discuss *Vedanta*. He was constantly thinking about the people groaning under the impact of the country-wide famine. He said, "pundit ji, first of all try to ameliorate the terrible distress that is prevailing everywhere, to still the heart-rending cry of your hungry countrymen for a morsel of food, after that come to me to have a dabate on the Vedanta. To stake one's whole life and soul to save thousands who are dying of starvation—this is the essence of the religion of the *Vedanta*."

On another occasion when Vivekananda was staying at the garden house of Cossipore a young man came to him and said,' "Swamiji, I have visited many places and have had intimate association with many religious sects, yet I find I do not as yet understand what Truth is. Everyday I close the door and sit in meditation, but peace remains as elusive as ever! Swamiji, tell me why?'

Swami Vivekananda patiently listened to him, then said: My child, if you want peace, you have to do exactly the opposite of what you have been doing so long. You have to keep your door open, you have to look around. If you do, you will be surprised to find how many people are anxiously waiting for your help. Help them, feed them, give them water to drink—serve them as much as you can. I guarantee, you will get peace."

Shri Girish Chandra Ghose, Shri Ramakrishnas householder disciple had once remarked upon the qualities of love and companion for humanity that governed Vivekananda and said, 'Did you notice what a great heart your Swamiji has? I love and respect Swamiji not because he is well versed in the Vedas and Vedanta but because of his infinite love and his rediness to share the sufferings of others."

After his hard work in the West, Vivekananda decided to reste for a while at Darjeeling, a hill station in the Himalayas. His rest was, however, cut shot by a sudden outbreak of plague in Calcutta.

He called his brother monks and his disciples together. “We shall go and nurse these sick people,” he said “We shall open a hospital, and we ourselves shall nurse those who have this awful disease.”

‘But, Swamiji, where is the money to do such work?’ some one asked.

'Money?’ The swami thundered.'Do not bother yourself about money. Get on with this work of service, if I have to, I shall sell the new *Math* and give all the money for his work!’ he continued; ‘Do you not remember that Sri Ramakrishna told us that we should serve God in man? This is service to God in man.’ It must be done. But he did not have to sell the *Math*. Money came and the work was done. The plague was over and people got well again.

At one time, there were some workmen at the *Math* who were called *Santhal*s. Vivekananda loved them very much. One of them was named Kesto.

‘Kesto,’ he said, ‘how would you like me to give you all a feast?’ Having saved them a big feast he said,’Today, I have fed God himself.

Shi Ramkrishna once admonished him when he asked for the bliss of super conscious state and the boon of remaining merged in that state, so that he could spend his life in absolute bliss. 'Shame on you! ‘Sri Ramakrishna said, ‘you are asking for such an insignificant thing, I thought that you would be like a big banyan tree and that thousands of people would rest in your shade. But now I see that you are seeking your own liberation.' Vivekananda was moved by his Master's words. It had a tremendous appeal to his heart. He was transformed completely. There after, the world saw Swami Vivekananda become a living symbol of the supreme ideal of dedicated service of God in man and in all. It was this Vivekananda who once cried out: 'May I be born again and again...and suffer thousands of miseries, so that I may worship the only God that exists, the only God I believe in, the sum totals of souls.' (C.W.S.V. Vol.V.P 137)

His Bengali poem *Sakhar Prati*, later translated into English under the caption *To a Friend*, speaks of the same experience.

This poem is the grand revelation of the Vedantic truth, perenial and eternal. He wrotes:

These are his manifold forms
Before thee,
Rejecting them, where seekest
Thou for God?
He is indeed serving God,
Who loves all beings.'(C.W.-IV. P. 496)

Swami Vivekananda knew that the key to *Nara Narayana Seva* was not just social work as we ordinarily mean, but to him, it was based on a purely spiritual vision. A highly God intoxicated person, Mahatma Gandhi, has borrowed the term *Daridra Narayana Seva* from Swami Vivekananda and popularised it.

After he returned from the West in 1897, Swami Vivekananda organised the name Ramakrishna Order in both monastic and a philanthropic aspect. To the philanthropic aspect he gave the name Ramakrishna Mission. Its purpose was for the monks and the laity to combine together to render all kinds of service, not only to the people of India but to people everywhere, and this not merely in the spirit of humanitarianism but in the spirit of worship, recognising the supreme truth that man is God Himself.

"I believe in helping the miserable. I consider that the great national sin is the neglect of the masses, and that is one of the causes of our down fall."(C.W. V-p 52& 227)."

3

Swami Vivekananda: A Social Reformer and Activist

Swami Vivekananda was not only a social reformer and a social activist but was also a saint (*swami*),a patriot, a poet, a spiritual teacher, a philosopher, a humanist, an educationest, a Vedantist, a sociologist and an orator also.

As a social reformer Swami Vivekananda made attempts to up-lift the common mass from ignorance, bondage, blind belief, superstitions etc. He said "bondage brings only misery. Desire, ignorance and inequality is the trinity of bondage. [9] Superstition is a great enemy of man, but bigotry is worse, if superstition enters, the brain is gone.[10] Do not run after these superstitions. Better for you and for the race that you became rank atheists, because you would have strength, but if these are degradation and death, Shame on humanity that strong men should spend their time in inventing allegories to explain the most rotten

---

9 C.W.Vol. VIII-p 414, p344.

10 Ibid-Vol-I, p. 15

superstitions of the world. Be bold, do not try to explain everything that way. The fact is that we have many superstitions, many bad spots and sores on our body—these have to be excised, cut off, and destroyed—but these do not destroy our religion, our national life, our spirituality!(C.W.Vol.3 p.279)."

Swami Vivekananda observed that the illiterate people observed peculiar systems of superstitions to worship the Gods. The educated and rational man should avoid all superstitions, omen, and blind beliefs. Every system which makes us superstitious, makes one weak and mope that must be completely avoided.

Being a reformer he used to say "if you wish to be a true reformer, three things are necessary. The first is to feel. Do you really feel that there is so much misery, so much ignorance and superstition in the world? Do you really feel that all the men are your brothers? Are you full of that idea of sympathy ? If you are, that is only the first step. You must think next if you have found any remedy. The old ideas may be all superstitions, but in and round these masses of superstition are nuggets of gold and truth. Have you discovered means by which to keep that gold alone, without any of the dross? If you have done that, that is the only second step; one more thing is necessary. What is your motive? Are you sure that you are not actuated by greed of gold, by thirst for fame or power? Are you really sure that you can stand to your ideals and work on, even if the whole world wants to crush you down? Are you sure you know what you want and will perform your duty, and that alone, even at your and life is at stake? Are you sure that you will persevere so long as life endures so long as there is one pulsation left in the heart? Then you are real reformer." (C.W.Vol. IV. P I59).

Three factors, in fact, superstition, ignorance, and poverty revolted Vivekananda against the so called religion and blossomed into his heart a great flame by which he has discovered the dark days of mankind. He wanted such a religion that could restore the distress of the people on the one hand and help to disseminate education to the destitute on the other hand. He represented not any particular sect or creed in the Parliament of Religions at Chicago, but represented human masses. He said" I am of the people I am a preacher of the people, I am a worker among the masses and my heart calls me there.[11] "(Madras Times, Feb 8,1897)

This is how Vedantic humanism transformed Vivekananda into a socialist and democratic of the highest order. This is how he discovered a relationship between God and man testifying the fact evidently that religious

11 Madras times, Feb, 8, 1897 and Eternal Platform, Editor Swami Vivekananda, RamaKrishna Mission Ashrama, Bankure, W.Bengal, 1993, "Swami Vivekananda: More than a Socialist"-by A.K. Sinha. Page. 122.

humanism was God-oriented and man-oriented. He went further and put up his theory declaring firmly that religious humanism is not merely sought to mitigate the sufferings of the common people but looked upon them as the manifestation of God. His whole religion is not doctrines or dogmas or rituals or books or temple or forms but the manifestation of divinity within. Hence he say 'Each soul is potentially divine.' (C.W.Vol.I.p 257).

Swami Vivekananda learnt from Shri Ramakrishna the tire great lesson *'Jato Mat Tato path'* (As many creeds, so many paths) and he emphasied the democratic spirit even in the matter of spirituality. Swami Vivakananda and Shri Ramakrishna cannot be considered to be mere religious leaders as they are commonly looked upon. They were far greater than that. They were prophets of human emancipation, of equality and of human progress. Their beliefs are clearly reflected when Ramakrishna says, "There is no religion in an empty stomach' or when Vivekananda says, "I do not believe in that God or in that religion that cannot wip out the tears of a widow or cannot give bread to a hungry mouth, or the only God l believe in is He whom the ignorant call man.'

Religion is not anti-moral but it is for the well-being of mankind. There is no mystery in religion. The purpose of religion is manmaking. Vivekananda said, 'religion is the manifestation of divinity already in man. Religion is not the outcome of the weakness of human nature, religion is love, unfolding, expanding, growing. It is in love that religion exists and not in (ceremony'(C.W.Vol.III P.4l). "The only medium through which spiritual force can be transmitted is love. This love makes the whole universe one's own home.)[12]"

Swami Vivekananda's conception of God was expressed through his love for humanity. His worship of God was identified with service of the masses, worship means love and means service with dedication. His love for the Indian masses and worship of God became the service of Mother India. His religion did not make him an austere Sannyasin shunning human society and expanding his energy in spiritual exercises for personal salvation, the *Mukti* or *Moksha*. On the contrary his religion opened his heart to the floodgates of love and compassion for his country men, who were suffering from poverty and disease, ignorance and superstition.

Swami Vivekananda cried and felt pity for the condition of the poor and the down-trodden. He said, 'remember that the nation lives in the cottage. But, alas! nobody ever did anything for them. Forget not the lower classes, the ignorant, the poor, the illeterate, the cobbler, the sweeper, are thy flesh and blood, thy brothers. Thou brave one, be bold, take courage, be proud that thou are an Indian, and

---

12 C.W. Vol-III. P 51 & Vol. V p78.

proudly proclaim , I am an Indian, every Indian is my brother. (C.W.IVP480).

Swami Vivekananda was really an epoch maker with a life span of less than forty years inspiring his brothers to fight against poverty, illiteracy, superstition, untouchability, priestcraft and tyranny of the wise. His mission had two major aspects: one worldmoving and the other nation making. In carrying out his mission he took inspiration from three great sources viz. Sri Ramakrishna, Mother-India and the masses.

Vivekananda's contribution to the awakening of modern India is unique in its quality and variety. In his wanderings as a *parivrajaka* from the Himalayas to Kanyakumari, he mixed with all classes of people, ate and slept with them, shared their joys and sorrow. His heart always throbbed with the masses and in their degradation he found himself humiliated, he vehemently criticised the orthodox, brahmanical caste system and viewed 'untouchability' as a type of mental disease of upper classes.

A study of his life will easily reveal that he was never a visionary who spent all his time in contemplation and meditation. He was a very practical and work-oriented person; *Karma Yogi*. He worked day and night organising relief centres, monasteries, *maths*, orphanages, hospitals and school for the betterment of the society. Throughout his life, he was a social activist following the ideals of renunciation and service. He always looked upon work as worship of God.

The central evils against which he fought were racialism, imperaliasm, communalism and untouchability. He held in high esteem the noble virtues like manliness, honour and dignity of the individual.

The social service of Swami Vivekananda was not only a physical help but a mission with attitude of rendering selfless service. According to him there should be purification in the worker's mind arousing consciousness of God in the object of service and spiritualisation of action, thereby elevating it to the level of divine manifestation. Similarly servicer to a fellow human being endeared with companion and devotion as a living diety takes the form of worship.'

Swami Vivekananda said, 'Helping others physically, by removing their physical needs is indeed great, but the help is great accordingly as the need is greater accordingly as the help is far reaching. If a man's wants can be removed for an hour, it is helping him indeed, if his wants can be removed for a year, it will be more help to him; but if his wants can be removed forever, it is surely the greatest help that can be given to him. It is only with the knowledge of the spirit that the faculty of wants is annihilated for ever; so helping man spiritually is the highest help that can be given to him. Next to spiritual comes intellectual help. The gift of knowledge is a far higher gift than that of food and clothes, it is even higher than giving life to a man, because the real life of man consists of knowledge. Life is of very little value, if it is a life in the dark, groping through ignorance and misery. Next in order comes, of course, helping a man physically'(C.W.Vol.I.p-52).

In 1898 there was a plague in Calcutta. People did not know what to do. Government promulgated several rules and regulations but there was nobody to explain them to the people. People were not only dying but they were in terror, panic and confounded. Swami Vivekananda had arrived from the West and was literally being worshipped. But he saw this Divine in the form of man succumbing to this calamitous situation. He plunged heart and soul into this work of bringing succour to people by undertaking programmes of cleanliness, hygiene, education distribution of medicine, serving the people physically by attending to them and nursing etc. with full concentrated devotion as he saw the manifestation of same Divinity in them. He was helped by the other disciples of Sri Ramakrishna and his own disciples. Soon the mist cleared, people became assured, sanity took over and the rot passed over. Since then in every natural calamity like storm, flood, famine, earthquake, fire etc. the Ramakrishna Mission has strived to bring succour to people whom it considers to be Narayana worshipped.

Swami Vivekananda, however, said that 'the miseries of the world cannot be cured by physical help only. Until man's nature changes, these physical needs will always arise, and miseries will always be felt, and no amount of physical help will cure them completely. The only solution of this problem is to make mankind pure. Ignorance is the mother of all the evil and all the misery we see. Let men have light, let them be pure and spiritually strong and educated, then alone will misery cease in the world, not before. We may convert every house in the country into a charity asylum, we may fill the land with hospitals, but the misery of man will still continue to exist until man's character changes (C.W.Vol 1.53).'

We have read in the *Bhagavad Gita* that we must all work incessantly. All work is, by nature, composed of good and evil. We cannot do any work which will not do some good somewhere; there cannot be any work which will not cause some harm some where. Every work must necessarily be a mixture of good and evil yet we are commanded to work incessantly. Good and evil will both have their results, will produce their Karma. Every act has its own positive and negative aspects and each aspect will produce its own results, or *Karma.*[13] Good action will entail upon us a good effect and bad action bad effect. But good and bad are both bondage of the soul. The solution reached in the Gita in regard to this bondage producing nature of work is that if we do not attach our selves to the work we do, it will not have any binding effect on our soul.

13 C. W. Vol-1. p. 53.

We shall try to understand what is meant by his non-attachment to work. 'This good and bad is, however, a bondage of the souls. According to the Gita.[14]

This is the central idea in the Gita; "work incessantly, but be not attached to it. Be unattached and do not bind yourselves because bondage is terrible. To attain this unattachment is almost a life-work, but as soon as we have reached this point we have attained the goal of love and become free."[15]

Karma yoga, therefore, is a system of ethics and religion intended to attain freedom through unselfishness, and by good works. Everything around us is trying to get freedom, flying away from bondage. This freedom is indeed the goal of *Karma yoga*. The work or service for the good of others leads to this state of *Jivanmukti*.

According to Swami Vivekananda, "one must be unattached to action and works for work's sake, if a man works without any selfish motive, he gains the highest."

(*Karma Yoga* is selfless service unto humanity. The important point is that you will have to serve humanity without any attachmant or egoism. A *Karma Yogi* should have a large heart. He should be free from crookedness, meanness, miserliness and selfishness. He should be

---

14 Ibid-p. 53.

15 Ibid-p. 59.

absolutely free from greed, anger and egoism. He should have an amiable, loving social nature.)[16]

A *Karma Yogi* purifies his heart through constant selfless or disinterested service. He works without expectation of fruits. He feels that he is a *Nimitta* or an instrument in the hands of the Lord. He also feels that the whole world is a manifestation of the Lord and that the whole world is He himself. Service of country, service of the society, service of the poor, service of sick, service of parents, service of the Guru and Mahatma are all *Karma Yoga*. Man is the manifestation of God. Service is altruism or humanitarianism for them.

(In the practice of the *Karma Yoga*, one can serve with mind and body, work is worship, serve everyone with intense love, without expect any fruits or reward. Service to humanity is service to God. Work elevates when done in the right spirit without attachment or egoism. The man who serves the world really serves himself. The man who helps others, really helps himself. Take delight in service. One can attain purity of heart through constant selfless service. Your minds be fixed in the Lord while your hands are in the service of humanity.)[17]

---

16 'Synerginslilutonline.com.' The author 'riteshtripathi 81' and this was posted on 31Aug, 2007.

17 www.dlshq.org.

We must discriminate whether one is working for himself, or for the good of others. If it be for the good of others, it is not with a selfish purpose. The work for work's sake that is the ideal. Do everything, or any thing for him only. And offer your fruits of action to him only. Remember that this body is the instrument of the true self.

"To work properly," according to Swami Vivekananda, "you have first to give up the ideas of attachment. Hold, yourself as a witness and go on working. To work without motive, to work unattached, brings the highest bliss and freedom. Yoga teaches; 'Do not give up the world. Live in the world and work incessantly like a stranger being unattached. Work only for the sake of doing work without desiring for its fruits!"

Swami Vivekananda said, "work like a master and not as a slave. The desire for name and fame with selfish motive is not good. Selfish work is slave's work. There are some people who work for work's sake, who do not care for name and fame or even to go to heaven. The world is created not for our enjoyment and not for our sake. The world is created for us, so also we are created for the world."[18]

According to Vivekananda, there are three qualifications of a *Karma Yogi*. 'First, feel for the heart. What is in the intellect or reason? It goes a few steps and

---

18 C.W - Vol. I. P. 88

there it stops. But through the heart comes inspiration. Love opens the most impossible gates. Love is the gate to all the secrets of the universe. The second is the practical solution to soothe the miseries of the people.[19] His philosophy of Vedanta was also practical one. He was a man of action and not of words. Thirdly, one must have the will to surmount mountain,-high obstructions. In addition to that, the attitude of doing service to the other should be like that of a humble servant, who would consider that to serve only he has the right and not to its consequence. It is work for work's sake, duty for duty's sake. It is *seva* or service, which is to be formed with humbleness, with all humility and reverence.

Service has been characterized by the *Bhagavad Gita* as *Sattvika*, *Rajasika*, and *Tamasika*. Actions are classified as *Karma*, obligatory action, in other words duty, then *Akarma*, in action and also *Vikarma*, forbidden action. Of these, duties or obligatory actions have to be performed at all times and in all places free from all attachment, and without the least care for their fruits. Vivekananda was a man of action. To him, only the *Rajasik* quality of a man is essential for vigrous and solid activities. The active state of mind is *Rajas*. *Rajas* is an activity, expressed as attraction or repulsion. *Tamas* is typified as darkness or inactivity, and *Sattva* is the equilibrium of the two.

---

19 Ibid-p. 88.

He said, 'The only true duty is to be unattached and work as free beings, to give up all work unto God. All our duties are His.' (C.W.Vol.I.P.Io)

It is stated in the Gita, 'He who even while doing action can keep his mind calm and steadfast in all circumstances, with one's body, mind and soul, he indeed is the perfect worker, the Yogi' (Gita,lV.18).

This idea must be preached to everyone—work, work, endless work—without looking at results, and always keeping the whole mind and soul steadfast at the Lotus Feet of the Lord; this is the central idea of the *Gita* according to Swami Vivekananda.

The ultimate goal of all mankind, the aim and end of all religions, is but one, re-union with God. But while the aim is one, the method of attaining may vary from man to man. Every man must develop according to his own nature. Different forms of Yogas, have been classified under four heads:

Karma Yoga-(communion through action)—The manner in which a man realises his own divinity through works and duty.

A deep penetrative study of the eventful life and the glorious deeds of the great Swami Vivekananda reveals his wonderfully generous and broad heart and his profoundly deep feelings for all irrespective of any distinction. Some of his illustrious utterances that he declared-' May I be born again and again and suffer thousands of miseries, so that I may worship the only God that exists, the God I believe in—the sum total of all souls- and, above all, my God, the wicked, my God, the miserable, my God, the poor of all races, of all species, is the special object of my worship. (C.W.Vol.Vp.136)

As a social reformer and an activist has devoted and dedicated his heart and soul to arise, awake and inspire the common masses of India. He therefore, advised us to dedicate ourselves, to the service of '*Daridranarayana*' or' *Siva jyane jiva seva*' is the best form of worship.

4

Vivekananda and Mass Awakening

Swami Vivekananda's social philosophy and his practical approach to life was very pragmatic and humanistic, but his aim was always on God realisation. His concept of service or worship was ultimately culminated in the realisation of oneness, viz. God in man. He was very much interested in the upliftment of the masses. He said, "our mission is for the destitute, the poor and the illiterate peasant and labouring classes. The peasant, the shoemaker, the sweeper, and such other lower classes Indian have much greater capacity for work and self-reliance than you. They have been silently working through long ages, and producing the entire wealth of land, without a word of complaint. Very soon they will get above you in position."(C. W VII. 148))

"They are the back bone of the nation, in all countries. If these lower classes stop work, from where will you get your food and clothing? .... if the labourers stop work, your supply of food and clothes also stops. And you regard them as low class people and vaunt about a your own culture" (C.W.VII.p.148).

'Let new India arise in your place. Let her arise out of the peasants' cottage, grasping the plough; out of huts of the fisherman, the cobbler, and the sweeper. Let her spring from the grocer's shop, from beside the oven of the fritter-seller. Let her emanate from the factory, from marts, and from markets. Let her emerge from groves and forests, from hills and mountains. These common people have suffered oppression for thousands of years—suffered it without murmur, and as a result have got wonderful fortitude. They have suffered eternal misery, which has given them unflinching vitality. Living on a handful of grains, they can convulse the world, give them only half a piece of bread, and the whole world will not be big enough to contain their energy; they are endowed with the inexhaustible vitality of a *Raktabija*. And, besides, they have got the wonderful strength that comes of a pure and moral life, which is not to be found anywhere else in the world. Such peacefulness, such contentment, such love, such power of silent and incessant work, and such manifestation of lion's strength in times of action-where else will you find these! (C.W.Vol. VII p.327-28).

Swami Vivekananda, thus, became a living symbol or the supreme ideal of dedicated service to God in man, and in all masses. Mentioning the upliftment of the masses he said; "I will even go to hell if by doing so I can help my brothers."[20]

---

20 C.W. V. Vol III. P. 143.

Vivekananda was very much sure that through the service of the poor and downtrodden masses of India one could sincerely worship God and realise Him.

He said, "He who sees Shiva in the poor, in the weak; and in the diseased, really worship Shiva; and if he sees Shiva only in the image, his worship is but preliminary" (C.W. III.142).[21]

Swami Vivekananda said that, 'We as a nation have lost our individuality, and that is the cause of all mischief in India. We have to give back to the nation its lost individuality and raise the masses. India is to be raised, the poor are to be fed, education is to be spread, and the evil of priestcraft is to be removed. More bread, more opportunity for everybody! (C.W.IV.368) He also said' if we want to regenerate India, we must work for them. No amount of politics would be of any avail until the masses in India are once more avail until the masses in India are once more well educated, well fed, and well cared for.'(CW.V.222)

"Remember that the nation lives in the cottage. But alas! nobody ever did anything for them... the fate of nation depend upon the condition of the masses. Can you give them back their lost individuality without making them lose their innate spiritual nature?" [22] Swamiji said

---

21 Complete works of Shri Vevekananda. Vol-III .P. 142.

22 C.W. V. Vol V. P. 29.

emphatically this is to be done at any cost. The uplift of the women, the awakening of the masses must come first, and then only can any real good come about for the country, for India" (C. W. VI. 490).

Swami Vivekananda, as a humanistic philosopher and a social reformer was always thinking for the betterment of the poor and backward people of India.

Vivekananda had realised that until weaker and low class people were not well kept and maintained through proper education and nourishment the society could not developed. So he suggested very strongly that 'The only way of getting our divine nature manifested is by helping others to do the same. If there is inequality in nature, still there must be equal chance for all or if greater for some and some less- the weaker should be given more chance than the strong. In other words, a Brahmana is not so much in need of education as a *candala*. If the son of a Brahmana needs one teacher, that of a *candala* needs ten. For greater help must be given to him whom nature has not endowed with an acute intellect from birth, it is a madman who carries coals to Newcastle. The poor, the downtrodden, the ignorant- let these be your God. (C.W..VI.319)

He said to his disciples that 'My boys, if you have any respect for my words, the first thing I will advise you to open all the doors and windows of your room. In your quarter there are lots of poor people sunk in degradation and misery. You will have to go to them and serve them with your zeal and enthusiasm. Arrange to distribute medicines to those who are sick, and nurse them with all care, supply food to him who is starving, teach with as much as lies in you the ignorant, and you begin to serve your brethren in this wise, I tell you, my child, you surely get peace and consolation. (Remini-scences of Swami Vivekananda, p 330)

Swami Vivekananda had full conviction that if one felt for the miserable and look up for help definitely the help would come. One must struggle for the upliftment of the poor, the ignorant, the downtrodden and the opressed. He said, "for this noble venture one must need to have three things: the heart to feel, the brain to conceive, the hand to work."

According to Vivekananda the illiterate, the poor, the destitute and labouring people could be won over by love. However, the primary requirement was to make them feel the necessity of help and improvement and also know what their problem and conditions. Then only the mission of service could be fruitful and success. Therefore, the first duty was to educate the people, to enlight them and to provide more consciousness.

He said, 'A11 the wealth of the world cannot help one little Indian village if the people are not taught to help themselves. Our work should be mainly educational, both moral and intellectual. The only service to be done for our lower classees is to give them education, to develop their lost individuality. They are to be given ideas, the eyes to be opened to what is going on in the world around them; and then they will work out their own salvation. Every nation, every man, and every woman must work out their own salvation. Give them ideas that is the only help they require, and than the rest must follow as the effect. Our duty is to put ideas into their heads, they will do the rest. This is what is to be done in India.' (C.W.II.p.26)

Vivekananda said, 'suppose you start schools in India for the poor, still you cannot educate them, how can you? The boy of four years would better go to the plough or to work, than to your school. But if the mountain does not go to Mohammed then Mohammed can come to the mountain. Why should not education go from door to door, say I. If a ploughman's boy cannot come to education, why not meet him at the plough or at the factory, just where ever he is? Go along with him like his shadow (C.W.Vol.VIII.P-88 &89).

He said 'your duty at present is to go from one part of your country to another, from village to village, and make the people understand that mere sitting idly won't do any more. Make them understand their real condition and say, "O ye brotners, arise! Awake! How longer would you remain sleep!" Go and advise them how to improve their own condition, and make them comprehend the submime truths of the *Shastras* (scriptures), by presenting them in a lucid and popular way. Impress upon their minds that they have the same right to religion as the Brahmins. Initiate all, evendown to the *chandalas*, in these fiery Mantras. Also instruct them, in simple words, about the necessities of life, and the trade, commerce, agriculture, etc. (C.W.Vol.V.38I)

With the intention of extending a helping hand towards the poor and needy people, he said, "help, if you can but do not harm them? Break not, pull not anything down, but build, help, if you can; if not then fold your hands, and stand by and see things go on. Do not injure, if you cannot render help. Take man where he stands, and from there give him a life. What can you and I do? Do You think you can teach even a child? You cannot, the child teaches himself. Your duty is to afford opportunities and to remove obstracles." (C.W.Vol.II.p.384-85)

Swami Vivekananda wanted freedom of action for the well-being and growth of life. He said. 'Liberty of thought and action is the only condition of life, of growth and well being. Just as man must have liberty to think and speak, so he must have liberty in food, dress and marriage and in every other thing, so long as he does not injure others.

Swami Vivekananda expected that with all enthusiasm, and zeal one should help eradicate misery and poverty considering it to be a noble service to the *Daridra Narayana*. He said, "distribute medicine to those who are sick and nurse them with all care, supply food to him who is starving and teach, man-making education to the illiterate and, ignorant. Thus we have to go over the length and breadth of the nation, preaching the gospel of salvation, the gospel of help, the gospel of social raising up- the gospel of equality. (Reminiscences-p. 328)

"Then only will India awake, when hundreds of large hearted men and women, giving up all desires of enjoying the luxuries of life, will long and exert themselves to their utmost, for the well being of the millions of their countrymen who are gradually sinking lower and lower in the vortax of destitution and ignorance."(Swamiji's Letters.p324-325).

Swami Vivekananda said, "you must give your body, mind and speech to the welfare of the world. You have read *Matrudebo bhaba. Pitrudebo bhaba*—look upon your mother as God, look upon your father as God—but I say, *Daridra debo bhaba*, *Murkha debo bhaba*—the poor, the illiterate, the ignorant the afflicted—let these be your God. Know that service to these alone is the highest religion.(C.W.VI.288)

Swami Vivekananda always inspired the young men of India and wanted them to sacrifice their life for the betterment of the masses. He believed that if only a few young and energetic young men with dedication and devotion could do any noble work and for them nothing was impossible. He had confidence on the couragious and brave young men of our country who, he said, must have the character of Mahavira as their ideal.

He said 'Be a hero. Always say, I have no fear. Fear is death, fear is sin, fear is hell, fear is unrighteousness and fear is wrong life. All the negative thoughts and ideas that are in this world have proceeded from this evil spirit of fear. He thus said, "work among those young men who can devote heart and soul to this one duty - the duty of raising the masses of India. Awake them, unite them, and inspire them with this spirit of renunciation; it depends wholly on the young people, of India '(C.W.V.78).

"This life is short, the vanities of the world are transient, but they alone live who live for others, the rest are more dead than alive. Have infinite patience and courage. Work for work only, for the good of others is life. He said, "be proud and proudly proclaim I am an Indian, every Indian is my brother, proudly proclaim at the top of the voice, "The Indian is my brother, the Indian is my life, India's gods and goddesses are my God, India's society is the cradle of infancy, the pleasure garden of my youth, the sacred heaven, the Varanasi of my old age." Say, brother, "The soil of India is my highest heaven, the good of India is my good and repeat and pray day and night. ("O Thou Lord of Gauri, Thou Mother of the Universe, vouchsafe manliness unto me !O Thou Mother of strength, take away my weakness, take away my unmanliness, and - Make me a Man !(C.W.Vol.IV480))

Swami Vivekananda's stress was on man himself, for given the right kind of man, no problem need be daunting. 'Man-making is my mission,' he used to say again and again. He said that the fate of the country can be determined by the common people. The masses possessed infinite power, but they were never given a chance to play their role in tackling national problems. He described the neglect of the masses as a national sin.

The masses remained mute spectators while the destiny of the nation was being decided by a handful of the so called intelligentsia who knew nothing about the problems of common people. In the vision of a new India, Swami Vivekananda wanted that the *sudras* (the working class people) should be on top. He wanted the working people to have opportunities enough to catch up with the intelligentsia of the country without the intelligentstia having to go down to make room for the working people. Thus he wanted a process of 'levelling up' and no 'levelling down.'

Swami Vivekananda said caste consciousness was a barrier to India's progress because at times casteism kills national consciousness. He said, we are orthodox Hindus, but we refuse entirely to identify ourselves with 'Don't-touchism.' That is not Hinduism, it is in none of our books; it is an orthodox superstition, which believed that religion lies in the kitchen and in the cooking pot. He strongly condemned conservatism and orthodoxy of higher caste people and the superstition and blind belief of the lower class people. In India caste hierarchy, sex inequality, untouchability and social taboos flourished because of the misinterpretation of religion.

In this process of awakening India and inspiring her people into a life of thought and action, the influence that Swami Vivekananda, the nation builder, has powerfully influenced the India of today. While Swami Vivekananda was fully conscious of the greatness of India and her invaluable possessions, he was not blind to her social and economic degradation. A real reformer that he was, he went to the very root of the problems and talked of our weakness and failings unsparingly. He pointed out that the present decadence of our country was due to various reasons, such as:

not taking inspiration from the past and working on those lines,

developing a very narrow isolationistic and restricted outlook with regard to other countries,

perversion of the life-current of her national existence-religion and

tyranny over the masses by the so called higher castes and the neglet of our women.

The important programme for the regeneration of India, according to him, was the uplift of her masses and women. The only solution that he gave for the uplift of the masses and the women was to impart to them the right sort of education. According to him, there was no problem that could not be solved by proper education. The education must be an eye-opener and the character -builder for man-making, in all matters.

Swami Vivekananda went to America and travelled twelve years all over India only for the awakening and upliftment of the common masses. He died at a premature age of thirty nine years only. His philosophy of humanism has been highly acclaimed by the people of India.

5

Mass Education–The Panacea

The working people, who has been kept aloof from in proper education since long, should now be given special attention for providing man-making education at any cost. The education should be made available to the common mass at their doorstep with necessary facilities and provisions. The only service to be done for our lower classes is to give them education to develop their individuality.

What is education? Is it book learning? No. Is it deverse knowledge? Not even that, is it only to provide information. Not at all. According to Swami Vivekananda "Education is the manifestation of the perfection already in man" (C.W.IV.P-358) "Education is not the amount of information that is put into your brain and runs riot there, undigested, all your life. We must have life-building, man-making, character making assimilation of ideas."(C.W.Vol.III.p302).

"We want that education by which character is formed, strength of mind is increased, the intellect is expanded, and by which one can stand on one's own feet."(C.W.V.342).

"The education which does not help the common mass of people to equip themselves for the struggle for life, which does not bring out strength of character, a spirit of philanthrophy, and the courage of a lion- is it worth the name? Real education is that which enables one to stand on one's own legs." (C.W.VII.PI47-I48).

"The very essence of education is concentration of mind, not the collecting of facts." [23] From the lowest man to highest yogi, all have to use the same method to attain knowledge. The more the power of concentration, the greater the knowledge that is acquired. One can develop the power of concentration through meditation and observing *Brahmacharya*. The Brahmacharin must be pure in thought, word and deed.

The object of the ideal system of education should not merely be the advancement of theoretical knowledge but also the advancement of life, development of highest powers and capacities, and also the unfoldment of the noblest potentialities of the student. He must be to apply, intelligently, to his own life all the ideas that he has learnt and gathered and thus promote his growth – physically, intellectually, morally and spiritually. Thus education which should aim at the development of the entire personality of man.

---

23 C.W. V. VI.p 38.

The self-realisation is possible only through 'education which is the manifestation of perfection already in man.' The attainment of perfection brings out the divine nature. The goal of human existence is to manifest the perfection and divinity of the soul. The complete system of education, as has been stated, implies a balance and harmony between the properly developed body, mind, and soul. "In our attempt at formulating the right type of education," according to Swami Vivekananda, "we have to regard life as an indivisible whole, and as such we have to include in our system of education both intellectual knowledge and spiritual realisation." He said 'look upon religion, as the innermost core of education'. Religion ought to be the basis of the education because spiritual realisation and religious education are the highest goal of our life.

The highest goal of life could be attained usually by passing through the various stages of life, one after another. The first stage of our life is *Brahmacharya*, which is very pertinent in connection to the perfection of education. Curing the period of studentship, the foundation of life is to be laid properly. That is the reason why great stress is given to the *Brahmacharya stage*.

The power of concentration is the only key to the treasure-house of knowledge. One can increase the power to concentrate by observation of strict *Brahmacharya*. The *Brahmacharins* must be pure in thought, word and deed. A

Brahmachari can transform the textual energy into spiritual energy.

Shradha and faith in our own selves must be reawakened and then only all the problems which face our country will gradually be solved by ourselves. What makes the difference between man and man is the difference in the *shradha* and nothing else. What makes one man great and another weak and low is this *shradha*. First have faith in yourselves. Faith is the most potent factors of humanity.

We are what our thoughts have made us. If a man thinks good thoughts and does good works, the sum total of impressions will be good and they in a similar manner will force him to do good. It is only by doing good to others that one attains one's own good, and it is by leading others to *Bhakti* and *Mukti* that one attains them oneself. Vivekananda said it is preferable to live on grass for the sake of doing good to others.

All knowledge that the world has ever received comes from the mind. All knowledge and all power are within. All knowledge comes from the human soul. Man manifests knowledge, discovers it within himself, which is pre-existing through eternity. Within man is all knowledge, and it requires only an awakening, and that much is the work of the teacher. You cannot teach a child any more than you can grow a plant. The plant develops its own nature. The child also teaches itself.

We want that education by which character is formed, good habits are manifested and personality is properly shaped to a greater extent. The ideal of all education, all training should be this man-making. The end goal of all education is to make the man grow. True education means an all-round culture—physical, intellectual, moral, and spiritual. A complete system of education implies a balance and harmony between the properly developed body, mind and soul. The physical body is to be sustained by proper material food, the mind to be developed through the assimilation of the right type of ideas, and the soul, to be nourished by earnest prayer and meditation.

The question arises, 'why should religion be associated with education at all.' The answer is obvious as Swami Vivekananda has declared that each soul is potentially divine, and the goal is to manifest this divine within' (C.W.Vol.I.124). He defined religion as 'the manifestation of the divinity already in man' (C.W.Vol.4.p.358). So also 'education which is manifestation of perfection already in man.' The attainment of perfection brings out the divine nature. As we know, the spiritual realisation as the highest goal of life and makes all secular knowledge subservient to it. Thus Swami Vivekananda had in mind that religion should be the firm foundation on which the great edifice of education was to be built. He said; 'I look upon religion as the innermost core of education.'(C.W.Vol.5.23I)

In imparting religious education to the students, stress is to be laid on the essentials of one's faith, viz, the nature of the soul, its relation to the supreme spirit and its attitude towards other souls. This is the basic common factor connecting all religions. The rituals and ceremonies which differ widely among religions, are not the essential parts of the true religion. "Religion is not in doctrines, in dogmas, nor in intellectual argumentation, it is being and becoming, it is realisation."(C.W.Vol.II P.43))

The only service to be done for our lower classes is to give them education, to develop their lost individuality, and to provide sufficient awakening by which they can live as civilized persons. The education that we are getting now is not a man-making education, it is merely a negative education of certain facts. Education is not about the amount of information or about obtaining degrees only but it must give a scope to stand on one's own feet.

There are certain conditions necessary in the taught and also in the teacher. The condition necessary for .the taught are purity, a real thirst after knowledge, and perseverance. Purity in thought, speech and act is absolutely necessary, in regards to the teacher we must see that he knows the spirit of scriptures viz. Vedas, Bible and Korans. The second condition necessary for the teacher is sinlessness. The teacher must be perfectly pure of heart and soul. then comes the value of his words. The third condition is in regard to the motive. The teacher must not teach with any ulterior selfish motive for money, name or fame. His work must be simply out of love, out of pure love for mankind at large.

"Our great national sin is the neglect of the masses and that is the cause of our downfall. No amount of politics would be of any avail until the masses in India are once more well educated, well fed and well cared for."(C.W.V.222-23)

The chief cause of India's ruin has been the monopolising of the whole education and intelligence of the land among a handful of men. If we are to rise again, we shall have to do it by spreading education among the masses. Mass education is the only solution to our different problems. Vivekananda proclaimed that by any means education must reach every home. Kindle their knowledge with the help of modern science. The medium of instruction must be in their mother tongue It would be better to narrate stories about different nation and culture during their leisure time. Tell them and make them understand, 'you are our brothers, a part and parcel of our bodies.' If they receive this sympathy from you, their enthusiasm for work will be increased a hundredfold.'

It was Swami Vivekananda who took the initiative to propagate the immediate need for a renewal of the ancient Indian education system. He could perceive the irrelevance and harmful effects of the western education which was taking roots and spreading its tentacles in the Indian soil.

However, Swami Vivekananda also recognised its positive aspects.

We should also realise that the principal aim of education should be the realisation of the relation that exists between the individual soul and the universal spirit. Education should always help the individual to acquire a complete integrated vision of life. Self-realisation and self-confidence should be the goal of education. Education does not mean acquiring intellectual sharpness alone, it implies spiritual growth and all-round reading of books does not achieve this.

True education can only be acquired under a true teacher. A teacher must be a living example which will definitely change the whole character of the student by moulding his career according to the 'ideal' which is before him. Thus moral training should form an important part of proper education.

Swami Vivekananda had a precise and clear conception of education. He insisted on the fact that education can help us in character building, and as a result of which strength on the mind. The intellect is expanded and which instils confidence in us to stand our own feet. But the ultimate goal of life and education should be to help each one to manifest the potential divinity within, that is, spiritual realisation. With this spiritual realisation one can dedicate oneself to the service of one's suffering fellow-men.

One has to realise that the need of the hour is not confined to one's own self only but to serve our fellow-men through our educational ability with a service motive. The importance of what we call non-formal adult education, today, was realised by Swami Vivekananda in his lifetime. He was also strongly in favour of a residential programme of education based on the model of the *'gurukula'* that is *'ashrama patha shala.'* The ideal educational campus would include workshops, farms, and factories to impart to the students technical and vocational training. However, his emphasis in education was always on subjective transformation rather than acquisition of information. He stressed on the need for freedom and discipline for the proper growth envelopment of the students.

For 'man-making and Character-; building education' of Swami Vivekananda, it is highly essential to introduce moral education in the Present System of education. In every field, the nation can be advanced if by spreading education among the masses is possible.

6

Renunciation and Service

Swami Vivekananda's love for the poor and downtrodden is legendary. (He said: "May I be born again and again, and suffer thousands of miseries, so that I may worship the only God that exists, the only God I believe in, the sum total of all souls—and above all, my God the wicked, my God the miserable, my God the poor of all races, of all species, is the special object of my worship."[24]

To Swami Vivekananda, the only God to worship was the human soul, in the human body. Of course, all animals are temples too, but man is the highest. This is the only God that is awake, our own race, every where his hands, everywhere his feet, everywhere his ears, he covers everything. When we have worshipped the *Virat*, we shall be able to worship all other gods.

We can serve or worship our countrymen only if we have the capacity of renunciation. When the human soul draws back from the material things of the world and tries to go into deeper things, when man understands that one

24 C.W.V-V-p 137.

day everything would be destroyed and to be reduced almost into mere matter, then only begins the renunciation. The *Karmayogi's* renunciation is the shape of giving up all the fruits of his action, he is not attached to the results and he does not care for any reward. The whole gist of teaching is that you should work like a master and not as a slave. Work incessantly, but renounce its fruits, work through freedom and work through love.

The main effect of work done for others is to purify ourselves and to avoid ego. The renunciation of sense pleasure is essential in the pursuit of *Bhakti*. Then the love of God increases, then the worldy desires and attachments to material objects gradually vanish and thrown aside and ultimately only the divine are consciousness prevails over the devotee. To Sri Ramakrishnaparamhansa, *Kamini* and *Kanchana* were the obstracle of spiritual austerity. *Bhakti yoga* does not say 'Give Up,' it only says "Love, Love the highest I and everything low naturally falls off from him, the object of whose love as the highest. *Bhakti*'s renunciation is that *vairagya* or non-attachment for all things that are not God which results from *Anuraga* or great attachment to God.

The *Jnana yogi* has the harshest of all renunciation to go through as he has to realise from the very first that the whole of this solid looking nature is all an illusion. The *Jnana yoga* is the high philosophy of life, the *jnani* aims at the wholeness of things, the absolute, the real, the

Barahman. Higher knowledge is the knowledge of *Brahman*. The *jnani* has to be free from all forms. To Swami Vivekananda, all knowledge and all power are within and not without, all knowledge is within us, it is in the soul, the goal of all is the realisation. of the self. Renunciation alone is the real secret of all realisation. Alpha and omega of *Vedanta Philosophy* is to 'give up' the world, giving up the unreal and taking the real.

"Service is the medium in and through which renunciation manifests itself. In fact, renunciation is the soul and its body. None can realise what renunciation is until and unless one finds its expression in and through selfless service. Service without renunciation is lifeless and renunciation without service is meaningless. Renunciation without service is a soul without a body and service without renunciation is a body without a soul. Service without renunciation, therefore, is no service at all but self-service. Service and renunciation are in reality one and the same. Service is not an act of charity, it is in reality an act of love, pure and selflees, done in regardless of consequences."[25]

According to Mahanarayana Upanishad, (12-14) 'Neither by progeny, nor by wealth, nor by performances of sacrifices but by renunciation alone, one can attain to

---

25 Vivekananda; Great Spiritual Teacher, Advaita Ashrama, Calcutta, 1995 p 412.

immortal bliss.' Bhagavan Sri Krishna eloquently proclaims the same idea when he declares his decree to his beloved disciple, Arjuna, in the following illustrious lines; "Better indeed is the knowledge than *abhyasa*; meditation is more esteemed than knowledge than meditation, the renunciation of the fruit of action is better, peace immediately follows renunciation.' (Gita-12-12). To Swami Vivekannda, renunciation is (the stepping stone and the real centre and the real heart of all spiritual culture. Through renunciation alone this immortality is to be reached, and goal can be achieved, here will be no spiritual strength unless one renounces the world. Swamiji also said that "if you desire to attain God, you will have to renounce *Kama-Kanchana* (Lust and possession)." (S.V.C.W.III.451))

"Service is of various kinds based on it is ministered on different planes in different times and places - physical or material, intellectual or educational, social or national and moral or religious. It holds a very high place in every sphere of human life, particularly religious. In India, from the very prehistoric period, if we look back to the Upanishadic age, which Buddhistic period is an echo, we come across many a reference to service.

"Service has been characterised by the Bhagavad Gita as *Sattvika, Rajasika,* and *Tamasika*. Actions are classified as *Karma*, obligatory action, in other words duty, then *Akarma*, in-action and also *Vikarama*, forbidden action. Of these duties or obligatory actions have to be performed at all times in all places free from all attachment, and without the least care for their (fruits; and relinquishing action in anticipation of physical troubles and painfulness is *Rajasika* and yields no result, whereas, abandonment of the same out of delusion is *Tamasika* and can never be tolerated. Men, who are born with divine attributes *(daivi prkriti)* which are marked by non-injury, truth, absence of anger, renunciation, tranquillity, absence of calumny, compassion to beings, non-covetousness, gentleness, modesty and absence of fickleness, are really the salt of this earth. Non-injury and compassion to all beings, irrespective of any distinction, are two of the most noble characterstics of the holy life." (Vivekananda: The Great spiritual Teacher, p 413)[26]

Work, whether good or bad, is always determined by its motive and the attitude with which the particular motive is realised. Work with motive does not come within our view of service, for service is always pure and selfless. The attitude of one doing service to other (*sevaka*) should be like that of a humble servant, who would consider that to serve only he has the right and not to its consequence, it is work for work's sake, duty for duty's sake.[27]' It is *seva* or service, which is to be performed with humbleness,

26 Ibid. P. 413.

27 Op. Cit. P. 415.

with all humility and reverence. He should be conscious of the fact that service *(seva)* is not *daya*, or an act of kindness or a compassion. An act of kindness or compassion *(daya)* has in it that proud sense of superiority from which *seva* (selflees service), is absolutely free. The *Sevaka* feels grateful to the man whom he serves and thinks that it is he *(sevya)* who has kindly agreed to give him the opportunity of practising selfless service which is regarded as an act of virtue. (Swami Vivekananda: The Great spiritual 'Teacher, sd, p.415).

"The national ideal of India" says Swami Vivekananda, "is renunciation and service." Upanishad declares, 'May your father be an object of worship to you. May your preceptor be an object of adoration to you." The great Swami Vivekananda added; "May the suffering millions be the object of worship to you, may the illiterate be the object of reverential service to you,"-(C.W.V.6,-p.288). This of course, is certainly not a departure from, but a development of the eternal ideas of service embedded in the scriptures.

Swami Vivekananda established the Ramakrishna Math and Ramakrishna Mission with the noble object of preaching and popularizing the spirit of renunciation and service. In the Ramakrishna Math the Sri Ramakrishna Order of monks used to stay with the observation of penances and austerities by developing the spirit of self-sacrifice which signifis stands for renunciation. The Ramakrishna Mission, which comprised in itself an endless variety of philanthropic activities stands for service. Their multifarious humanitarian activities, absolutely selfless in character, presents a veritable expression of service. As repeatedly declared by Swami Vivekananda, the order of Ramakrishna Math and Mission was to serve a double purpose-salvation of one's self and good of the world, *'Atmano-mokshartham jagad-dhitaya-ca.'*

The old ideal of selfless service has been handed down to posterity without any break through various religious ceremonies and festivals, in which acts of charity play everywhere a very important role. The spirit of service reaches its consummation when the *sevaka* (server) finds the same supreme self everywhere as the manifestation of *Brahman.* To Swami Vivekananda it is called *siva jyane jiva geya.* According to the *Vadanta* philosophy of Sankaracharya *jiva* and *Brahman* are identical. With this view in mind a server or a *sevaka* can serve mankind selflessly without the sense of ego.

According to Swami Vivekananda, the *Vedanta* does not, in reality, denounce the world. What it seeks to teach is the deification of the world and not its annihilation. It does not give us a suicidal advice to kill ourselves and annihilate the world. As per the *Ishopanishad* which says: 'Whatever exists in this universe, is to be cohered with the

Lord.' Vivekananda further says; 'you can have your wife, it does not mean that you are to abandon her, but that you are to see God in the wife. So also, you are to see God in your children. So in everything, in life and in death, in happiness and in misery, the Lord is equally present. The whole world is full of the Lord. Open your eyes and see him. This is what *Vedanta* teaches.' (Swami Vivekananda, Jnanayoga,p.140-41).

Swami Vivekananda's practical Vedanta, *Tat tvam asi* -'That Thou art-interprets that-'Every soul is potentially Divine. The goal is to manifest this Divine within by controlling nature, external and internal. His intense humanism also found expression in his doctrine of practical *Vedanta*. He maintained that fundamental *Doctrine of Vedanta*, namely, the basic Divinity of the *jiva*, has a message for men in all stations of life.

According to him, "from the highest standpoint, self-realisation is self-manifestation. "He gives the meaning of life through strength and courage. He says: 'make your nerves strong, what we want is muscles of iron and nerves of steel. We have wept long enough. No more weeping, but stand on your feet, and be men"[28] 'One can serve the backward people with vigour and sound mind. He was a worshipper of the living God. He made God in the heart of all the sole objects of his worship. Even as a

---

28 C.W.V. III. P. 224.

child he would be overwhelmed to see the sufferings of the poor. He lived with the poor masses of India, slept with them, ate with them, cried for their material salvation. Service of this living God was the joy of his last days.

Swami Vivekananda said, 'those who serve the servants of God are His greatest servants. It is the greatest privilege in our life that we are allowed to serve the Lord in all these shapes. One cannot help anyone but can only serve. Blessed are they whose[29] bodies get destroyed in the service of others.' He had a very comprehensive view of the welfare of the world, especially of India. He aimed at the economic, social, moral and spiritual development of the people. He believed that the principles of *Vedanta*, if properly understood and applied in life, would bring about all round development of humanity. Like Prometheus, he brought down the spiritual power from heaven and made it spring up on earth in the hearts of all. This shifting of God from a far off heaven to the human heart, as our innermost self, marks a momentous advance in the spiritual history of the world.

Our duty to others means helping others, doing good to the world. Why should we do good to the world? Apparently, to help the world, but really to help ourselves. We should always try to help the world, that should be the

29 C.W.V.III p. 83, 142.

highest motive in us, but if we consider well, we find that the world does not require our help at all. This world was not made for you or I to come and help it, yet we must do good. The desire to do good is the highest motive power we have if we know all the time that it is a privilege to help others.

After much austerity he said, I have understood this as the real truth. "God is present in every *jiva,* there is no other God besides that." [30] Who serves *Jiva*, serves God indeed.' Seek your own self in every being that breathes and in every atom of the universe. When you realise this, you cannot live in this world without treating everyone with exceeding love and compassion. This is indeed practical *Vedanta*. This is the gist of all worship—to be pure and to do good to others. He who sees Shiva in the poor, in the weak and in the diseased, really worship Shiva, and if he sees Shiva only in the image, his worship is but preliminary.

To Swami Vivakananda betterment should start with the humblest of the humble first and therefore he had uppermost in his mind the *Daridra Narayana*—the God in the poor, "the only God that exists, the only God in whom I believe, my God the miserable, my God the poor of all races." [31] The hungry, down trodden of India must be

---

30 C.W.VII. p 427..

31 C.W.V. p. 137.

given back their lost self-confidence and sense of self-respect. They must be taught to realise that they too have some duty and responsibility in the country. So Social Service, in tone sense of the term is possible, only if one make renunciation in his way of life.

7

Philosophy of Humanism

Vivekananda's love for the country and the masses had its foundation in his philosophy of humanism, which in turn was rooted in his conviction that man is basically a divine spirit. His heart was buring with passionate desire to awaken the people of India. He used to say frequently, 'Arise, awake and stop not till the goal is reached." His heart was full of love and sympathy towards mankind. Love was the first and last word of his humanism.

The humanism expounded by Swami Vivekananda was intensely human and universal. His philosophy of humanism was based on the universal vision of man as the *Atman*. His humanism derived from the philosophy of man in depth, *adhyatma-vudya Vedanta*. In dealing with this profound truth about man, *Vedanta*, he, preferd to use the term unfoldment.

"The philosophy of man," according to Swami Vivekananda, "is to see God in everything. But if you cannot see him in everything, see him in one thing, in that thing you like best, and then see Him in another. So on you can go. There is infinite life before the soul. Take your time and you will achieve your end." (C.W.II.151-53)

Swami Vivekananda said we want to worship a living God. I have not seen anything but all my life, nor have you. To see this chair you first see God, and then chair in and through Him. He is everywhere, saying, 'I am', you are conscious of existence. Where shall we go to find God if you cannot see him in your own hearts and in every living being?' (Swami Vivekananda: Vedanta; voice of Freedom,pII4).

Vedanta says there is nothing that is not God. The living God is within you, and yet you are building churches, and temples and beliving all sotrs of imaginary nonsense. The only God to worship is the human soul in the human body. Of course all animals are temples too, but man is the highest. If I cannot worship in that, no other temple will be of any advantage. The moment I have realised God sitting in the temple of every human body, the moment I stand in reverence before every human being and see God in him, that moment I am free from bondage (Ibid.pII5).

All belongs to the Lord. *Vedanta* says to put God in everything and know him to be in everything. He is already in everywork, in every thought, in every feeling. If one can realise this then there is no problem. The sorrow, happiness, joy, suffeing, all these cannot touch our heart. But due to our ignorance, we thought we have lost something or gained some other thing. But the truth is that which is within us. It is free from everything. The man who has in this life attained this state, for whom, for a minute at least, the ordinary vision of this world has changed becomes a universal man.

We are infinite beings, this is the real nature of man. The body is not real man; neither the mind, for the mind waxes and wanes. It is the spirit beyond, which alone one can live forever. The body and mind are continually changing. One moment it is happy, another moment unhappy; one moment strong, another weak—an ever changing whirlpool. That cannot be the spirit, which is infinite. Change can only be in the limited. To say that the infinite change is absurd, it cannot be. So this infinite unit is unchangable, immovable and absolute.

Swami Vivekananda said that, "we are not individuals yet. We are struggling toward individuality, and this as the infinite, that is the real nature of man. He alone lives whose life is in the whole universe, and more we concentrate our lives on limied things, the faster we grow towards death, it is the God within your own self that is impelling you to seek for Him to realize him. After long searches here and there, in temples and in churches, in earths and in heavens, at least you come back, completing the circle from where you started, to your own soul, and find that He for whom you have been seeking all over the world, for whom you have been weeping and praying in churches and temples, on whom you were looking as the mystery of all mysteries, surrounded in the clouds, is the nearest of the near, is your own self, the reality of your life, body and soul. That is your own nature. Assert it, manifest it. You are not to become pure, you are pure already, you are not to become perfect; you are that already!" (Swami Vivekananda, Vedantas Voice of Freedom,P.119)

One idea stands out as the centre of all ethical systems, expressed in various firms—namely, doing good to others. The guiding motive of mankind should be charity toward men, charity toward all animals. But these are all various expressions of that eternal truth that "I am the universe; this universe is one." Or else, where is the reason? Why should I do good to my fellow men? Why should I do good to others? What compels me? It is sympathy, the feeling of sameness every-where.

Now let me explain the idea of the humanistic social philosophy of Swami Vivakananda in the following examples. In worshipping God we have been always worshiped our own hidden self, stated Swami Vivekananda. He also said that the worst lie that you can ever tell yourself is that you were born a sinner or a wicked man. He alone is a sinner who sees a sinner in another man. Suppose there is a baby here, and you place a bag of gold on the table. Suppose a robber comes and takes the gold away. To the baby it is all the same because there is no robber outside. So the wicked see this universe as a hell, and the partially good see it as heaven, while the perfect beings realise it as God Himself.

According to Swami Vivekananda, "*Vedanta* recognizes no sin. It recognizes only error. And the greatest error, says *Vedanta*, is to think that you are weak, that you are a sinner, a miserable creature, and that we have no power and you cannot do this and that. Therefore, whosover thinks he is weak is wrong; whosoever thinks he is impure is wrong and is throwing a bad thought into the world."(C.W.-II. P. 295)

The central ideal of Vedanta is oneness, we must not look down with contempt on others. All of us are going toward the same goal. The difference between weakness and strength is one of degree. The difference between virtue and vice is one of degree. The difference between heaven and hell is one of degree. The difference between life and death is one of degree. The differences in this world are of degree and not of kind, because oneness is the secret of everything. All is one, which manifests itself either as thought, life or soul or body, and the difference is only in degree.

If you can stretch out a helping hand, do so. If you cannot, fold your hands, bless your brother, let them go their own way. Dragging down and condemning is the way to work. Never is work accomplished in that way. We spend our energies in condemning others. Criticism and condemnation are a vain way of spending our energies, for in the long run we come to learn that all seeing the same thing, are more or less approaching the same ideal, and that most of our differences are merely differences of expression.

There may be weakness, says Vedanta, but never mind; we want to grow. The remedy for weakness is not brooding over weakness, but thinking of strength. 'Teach men of the strength that is already within them, never say no; never say."I cannot;" for you are infinite. Even time and space are as nothing compared with your nature. You can do anything and everything. You are Almighty.

Vivekananda gave a clarion call that, "You are the pure one. Awake and arise, o mighty one. This sleep does not befit you. Awake and arise, it does not befit you. Think not that you are weak and miserable. Almighty one, arise and awake, and manifest your true nature, it is not fitting that you think yourself sinner. It is not fitting that you think yourself weak." (C.W.S.V.-II,p.304).

The weak have no will and never work. He who always thinks of himself as weak will never become strong. There is only one sin. That is weakness. We suffer because we are weak. He become miserable because we are weak. Swami Vivekananda said "the problem of misery cannot be solved by the intellect, but through the heart. If all this vast amount of effort had been spent in making men purer, gentler, more forbearing, this world would have a thousand fold more happiness than it has today. Always cultivate the heart. Through the heart the Lord speaks, and through the intellect you yourself speak." (CWV.I.4I4)

In India the conception of Divinity in living beings is as old as the age of the *Veda*s. The Vedic seers realized the Absolute in the highest superconscious state and visualized him in and through all. The *Upanisad*s declare emphatically that one supreme *Brahman* pervades the whole Universe and is the sum total of all souls. The *Gita*, the *Bhagavatam*, the *Purana*s, the Epics and other Hindu scriptures sing equally of the noblest conception of an all-pervading *Brahman*. But the tragedy of things is that no serious attempt has been made by the people to translate this sublime doctrine into practical life. There has been some practical attempt made by Swami Vivekananda to worship human beings as God.

Swami Vivekananda not only expressed sympathy and compassion for the oppressed people, as did, at that, time many liberal reformers, who through partial reforms in the way of life sought somehow to ease the lot of their compatriots.

He declared further that God realisation is to be achieved through the service of afflicted humanity. He saw his God in man *'Nara'* or man and *'gana'* or the masses were to him *Narayana* (or the Lord Himself in flesh and blood).

One of the remarkable positive phenomena of the presentday world, a world wiser and more sober with the disillusionment of the age, has bean the renaissance of humanism in various odeological systems. Humanism has always emerged as a reaction to the treat to mankind. In the European Renaissance—to the threat of religious fanaticism in the Enlightenment—to tie threat from national chauvinism and the enslavment of man to the machine and economic interests. The revival of humanism in todays world is an outcome of the failure of the great premise of the industrial age on the one hand, and a quest for an authentic, civilised human society on the other.

Swami Vivekananda had so much vitality that even today for he belongs to the humanist mainstream of culture. His humanism was derived from the Indian cultural heritage, especially the philosophy of *Vedanta*. He was aware of the various deformations of modern industrial civilisation—the occult power of money, the hierarchy of status, egoism and the division of the personality into official and private compartments. He believed that the deformations could be eliminated by a new system of socialism with a human face. As an optimist he did not, however, reject this modern civilisation.

Essential to Vivekananda's view of man is the basic assumption of man's freedom and activity. According to this view one cannot say that a certain man is innately a coward or a sinner or a fool or knave. One can only say that he acts in a foolish way or in a cowardly manner or in a vicious manner, and by his actions attains the attributes of cowardliness or foolishness or viciousness and so on. Man is, on the countrary, pure, and free at all times. Every human being is perfect being.

Man is necessarily responsible for his actions; good or bad. He himself must answer for the consequences of his actions on himself, and on society. There is no higher power to whom he can go for refuse or excuse, no one to redeem him for being other than what he is. Responsibility lies squarley upon man's shoulders. Thus when Swami Vivekananda gives the clarion call,' "rise, thou the effulgent one, rise thou who art always pure, rise almighty one and manifest your nature," and when using a homely example, he said; "if the room is full of darkness, the task is not to weep and wail, it is to strike a match, to bring the light, to dispel darkness,' he refers to man's possibilities, and the responsibility he cannot escape.

We can classify his contributions to humanity under the following heads:

He taught us Vedanta in a new light.

He stressed upon the practice of religion of service based on selflessness.

He directly or indirectly influenced in awakening, building and organising modern India with its patriotic, spiritual and service movements.

He worked as a cultural and spiritual ambassador of India to the West.

He interpreted the Indian values in the universal language of science.

He contributed enormously to taming and unifying, various aspects of life and science.

8

Swami Vivekananda: Service is Worship

Swami Vivekananda was the worshipper of the living God. He made God in the heart of all the sole objects of his worship. Even as a child he would be overwhelmed to see the sufferings of the poor. To see God in all and serve Him became the passion of his youth, the dream of his wandering days.

He used to ask "Do you love your fellow men? Should you go to seek for God—are not all the poor, the miserable, the weak, Gods— why not worship them first? Why go to dig a well on the shores of the Ganga?" (S.V.C.W,V.51)

You have read, look upon your mother as God, look upon your father as God but I say, the poor, the illiterate, the ignorant, the afflicted—let these be your God.'(C.W-VI-p288)

He said, "I don't believe in God or religion which cannot wipe the widow's tears or bring a piece of bread to the orphan's mouth. However sublime be the theories, however well-spun may be the philosophy—I do not call it religion.'(C.W-V-p50)

"The crying evil in the East is not religion-they have religion enough-but it is bread that the suffering millions of burning India cry out for with parched throats. They ask us for bread, but we give them stones. It is an insult to a starving people to offer them religion; it is an insult to a starving man to teach him metaphysics."(C.W.V-I p20)

"He is ever manifest as love in all beings. What other Gods - the creation of your mind-are you then going to worship. Let the *Vedas*, the *Koran*, the *Puranas* and all the scriptural lumber rest now for some time- let there be worship of the visible God of Love and compassion in the country."(C.W.VI.41O)

"The secret of religion lies not in theories but in practice. To be good and to do good-that is the whole of religion. Be moral brave, be a heart-whole man. Strictly moral, brave unto desperation. Don't bother your head with religious theories. Cowards only sin, brave men never, no, not even in mind."(C.W.V.3)

If you are really pure, how do you see the impure? For what is within is without. We cannot see impurity within having it inside ourselves. This is one of the practicals of *Vedanta*.

Vivekananda said, "look upon every man, woman and every one as God. You cannot help anyone, you can only serve: serve the children of Lord, serve the Lord himself, if you have the privilege. If the Lord grants that you can help any one of His children, blessed you are that privilege was given to you when others had it not. Do it only as worship. I should see God in the poor, and it is for my salvation that I go and worship them. The poor and the miserable are for our salvation, so that we may serve the Lord, coming in the shape of the diseased, coming in the shape of the lunatic, the leper, and the sinner!" (CW.III.246-247)

The first of all worship is the worship of the *Virat* of those all round us, worship it. Worship is the exact equivalent of the sanskrit word, and no other english word will do. These are all our gods—men and animals; and the first gods we have to worship, instead of being jealous of each other and fighting each other." (C.W.III.30I)

It is said in the *Shastra* that those who serve the servants of the God are his greatest servants. By the power of this, the heart becomes pure and then Shiva, who is residing in every one, will become manifest and if a man is selfish, even though he has visited all the temples, seen all the places of pilgrimage, and painted himself like a leopard, he is still further off from Shiva.

Swami Vivekananda said, 'you are the highest temple of God, I would rather worship you than any temple, image, or Bible.... The only God to worship is the human soul in the human body. If I cannot worship in that, no other temple will be of any advantage. The moment I have realised God sitting in the temple of every human body, I stand in reference before every human being and see God. In him—that moment I am free from bondage, every thing that binds vanishes, and I am free!"(C.W.II-320-21)

People never stop to think that those who bestowed the least thought on their own individualities have been the greatest workers in the world. Then alone a man loves when he finds that the object of his love is not any low, little, moral thing. Then alone a man loves when he finds that the object of his love is not a clod of earth, but it is the veritable God Himself. The wife will love the husband the more when she thinks that the husband is God Himself. The husband also will love the wife the more when he knows that the wife is God Himself. The mother will love children more who thinks that the children are God Himself. That man will love his greatest enemy who know that the very enemy is God Himself."(My India, The India eternal p.I05)

We must think ourselves blessed for the privilege given to us of working for God, and not of helping Him, who comes in the forms of the poor, the miserable and the afflicted. The service of the distressed does not only assist the suffers in the mitigation of their sufferings but also helps their servers even more effectively in the realisation of the self. The giver is aways the recipient. If service is rendered in the true spirit of worship, it is the most efficious means to spiritual realisation, for man is the highest symbol of God and the service of man is the highest form of worship on earth.

However, one cannot serve the suffering humanity in the true spirit of worship without realising the inherent divinity in them. For this self realisation the constant practise in the spirit of worship will enable the server in due course of time. But that must not deter us from practising such noble mission of serving humanity.

Great work requires great and persistent effort for a long time. According to *Karma yoga* of *Bhagavad Gita*, the action one has done cannot be destroyed until it has borne its fruit; no power in nature can stop it from yielding its result. He works best who works without any motive neither for money, nor for fame, nor for anything else.

Advaita Vedanta philosophy declared that one supreme Being pervades the entire universe. It means there is nothing that is not God. The ideal of man is to see God in everything. The living God is within us that is to be realised. The man is potentially divine. "The goal is," according to Swami Vivekananda, "to manifest this divinity within. The one central ideal of *Vedanta* is oneness. We can have no conception of God higher than man, so our God is man and man is God. (C.W.VII.30)

In the field of moral development Swami Vivekananda's contribution is of inestimable value. He stressed upon two main moral principles—unselfishness and strength. Other than service, the virtue that Swami Vivekananda stressed upon most was strength and fearlessness. Strength is the one sovereign virtue that every man needs in every second of his life because, without it, it is impossible to practise any other virtue. We make so many pious resolutions to be good and virtuous but fail to carry them out because of the lack of strength of will strength is goodness, weakness is sin.' Strength is the root virtue; all other virtues are only branches, leaves, flowers and fruits. Explaining the importance of strength, Vivekananda, said; 'it is weakness, says *Vedanta*, which is the cause of all misery in this world. Weakness is the one cause of suffering, we become miserable because we are weak. We lie, steal, kill and commit other crimes, because we are weak. We die because we are weak. Where there is nothing to weaken us, there is no death, no sorrow.'

Although he gave great importance to physical strength and moral strength, real strength according to him is that which comes through the realisation of the true Self of man. Even a strong faith in the divinity of the self is enough to give one great strength. Swami Vivekananda's prime interest, therefore, was in the spiritual development of man. We should not forget that he was first and foremost a great spiritual luminary. He was a born Yogi, as his master Ramakrishna himself had said of him. Having scaled the highest peaks of spiritual experience, the natural tendency of his mind was to soar in the higher realm of the spirit. He could have remained alone absorbed in the bliss of the Supreme self, but his Master had commanded him to serve humanity.

The house holder is the centre of life and society. It is a worship for him to acquire and spend wealth nobley by good means for good purposes. Be good and have mercy on those who suffer, it is not so easy to be good. But at the same time it is too difficult to be bad, A person who serves the society should not think that because it is good action therefore he is doing it. Rather his service to the mankind should be automatic without having any desire or selfish interest, his service should be for the sake of service and not for anything else, this is the true service or true worship indeed.

See God in man. Who serves *jiva,* serves God indeed.' Serving man, knowing him to be the manifestation of God, purifies the heart, and in a short time the aspirant who does this realises that he is a part of God-Existence-Knowledge-Bliss-Absolute.

Swami Vivekananda has rightly said that '*Shiva Jyanne Jiva Seva.*' The only God to worship is the human soul in the human body. However, he did not deny the worship of the divine God and Goddess. He also said to the youth of our country, "Be proud that thou art an Indian and proudly proclaim I am an Indian, every Indian is my brother. Proudly proclaim at the top of thy voice, The Indian is my brother, the Indian is my life, India's gods and goddesses are my God, India's society is the cradle of my infancy, the pleasure garden of my youth, the sacred heaven, the Varanasi of my old age."

"Man, according to the *Vedanta* philosophy, is the greatest being that is in the universe, and this world of work is the best place in it, because only herein is the greatest and the best chance for him to become perfect. Angles or gods, whatever you may call them, have all to become men, if they want to become perfect. This is the great centre, the wonderful opportunity-this human life.

Vedanta teaches men to have faith in themselves first. The *Vedanta* says, "a man who does not believe in himself is an atheist." Not believing in the glory of our own soul is what the *Vedanta* calls atheism....it recognizes no sin, it only recognizes error, and the greatest error, says the *Vedanta*, is to say that you are weak, you are a sinner, a miserable creature, and that you have no power, and you cannot do this and that.

The old religions said that he was an atheist who did not believe in God. The new religion says that he is the atheist who does not believe in himself. Swami Vivekananda said 'I accept all religions that were in the past and worship with them all. I worship God with everyone of them in whatever form they worship Him. I shall go to the mosque of the Mohammedan; I shall enter the christian's church and kneel before the crucifix; I shall enter the Buddhistic temple, where I shall take refuge in Buddha and in his law. I shall go into the forest and sit down in meditation with the Hindu, who is trying to see the light which enlightens the heart of everyone. Not only shall I do all these, but I shall keep my heart open for all that may come in the future.'

A man ought to live in this world like a lotus leaf, which grows in water but is never moistened by water; so a man ought to live in the world- his heart to God and his hands to work. Man is to become divine by realising the divine. Do this either by work, or worship, or psychic control, or philosophy, by one or more, or all of these and be free.

9

Flashes from Swami Vivekananda on Social Philosophy

Our duty to other means helping others; doing good to the world. Why should we do good to the world? Apparently to help the world, but really to help ourselves. Helping others is only helping ourselves (C.W; V. I-p75).

You cannot help anyone, you can only serve; serve the children of the Lord, serve the Lord Himself, if you have the privilege, if the Lord grants that you can help anyone of His children, blessed you are; do not think too much of yourselves. Blessed you are that the privilege was given to you when others had it not. Do it only as a worship (C.W.III. p246).

Blessed are we that we are given the privilege of working for Him, not of helping Him. Cut out this word 'help' from your mind. You cannot help, it is blaspheming. You are here yourself at His pleasure. Do you mean to say, you help Him? You worship. When you give a morsel of food to the dog, you worship the dog, you worship the dog as

God, God is in that dog. He is in that dog. He is all and in all (C.W. V. p246).

To Swami Vivekananda,

'The good live for others alone, the wise man should sacrifice himself for others. I can secure my own good only by doing your good. There is no other way, none whatsoever (C.W-VI.p317).

Go from village to village, do good to humanity and to the world at large. Go to hell yourself to buy salvation for others. When death is so certain, it is better to die for a good cause (VI•265.67).

Throughout the history of the world, you find great men make great sacrificies and the mass of mankind enjoy the benefit. If you want to give up everything for your own salvation, it is nothing. Do you want to forgo even your own salvation for the good of the world? You are God, think of that (VI.280).

A, hundred thousand men and women, fired with the zeal of holiness, fortified with eternal faith in the Lord, nerved to lion's courage by their sympathy for the poor and the fallen and downtrodden, will go over the length and breadth of the land, preaching the gospel of salvation, the gospel of help, the gospel of social raising up-the gospel of equality (C.W,VI-15).

'In your quarter there are lots of poor people sunk in degradation and misery. You will have to go to them and serve them with your zeal and enthusiasm. Arrange to distribute medicines to those who are sick, and nurse them with all care, supply food to him who is starving, teach with as much as lies in you the ignorant, and if you begin to serve your brethren in this wise, I tell you, my child, you will surely get peace and consolation' (Reminiscences of Swami Vivekananda, p 330).

In one word, the ideal of Vedanta is to know man as he really is, and this is its message, that if you cannot worship your brother man, the manifested God, how can you worship a God who is ummanifested? (C.W-II. p325-26)

The *Vedanta* says, "there is nothing that is not God. The living God is within you, and yet you are building churches and temples and beliving all sorts of imaginary nonsense. The only God to worship is the human soul, in the human body, of course, all animals are temples too but man is the highest" (C.W-II. p32I).

"The only service to be done for our lower classes is to give them education, to develop their lost individuality. They are to be given ideas; their eyes are to be opened to what is going on in the world around them; and then they will work out their own salvation" (C.W-IV.362).

'My plans are... to reach these masses of India. We have to follow the plan laid down by our ancestors, that is, to all the ideals slowly down among the masses. Raise them slowly up, raise them to equality, impart even secular knowledge through religion' (C.W-V.p.2I3).

'Look upon every man, woman, and everyone as God. After so much austerity, I have understood this as the real truth—God is present in every *jiva;* there is no other God besides that. Who serves *jiva*, serves God indeed' (C.W. II. p326).

You must give your body, mind and speech to "the welfare of the world." You have read *'Matrudebo Bhava, Pitru Debo Bhava'*- look upon your mother as God, look upon your father as God"-but I say *'Daridra Debo Bhava, Murkha Debo Bhava'* the poor, the illiterate, the ignorant the afflicted- let these be your God. Know that service to these alone is the highest religion (C.W.VI.288).

Work among those young men who can devote heart and soul to this one duty of raising the masses of India. Awake them, unite them, and inspire them with this spirit of renunciation; it depends wholly on the young people of India (C.W.V. p78).

Make men first. Men we want, and how can men be made unless *Shradha* is there? Arise, awake; wake up yourselves, awaken others. Achieve the consummation of human life before you pass off-"Arise, awake, and stop not till the goal is reached" (C.W. VI.5I2).

This life is short, the vanities of the world are transient, but they alone live who live for others, the rest are more dead than alive (C.W. IV.480).

May I be born again and again and suffer thousands of miseries. So that l may worship the only God that exists, the God I believe in—the sum total of all souls—and above all my God the wicked, my God the miserable, my God the poor of all races, of all species, is the special object of my worship (C.W-V 136).

The miseries of the world cannot be cured by physical help only. Until man's nature changes, these physical needs will always arise, and miseries will always be felt, and no amount of physical help will cure them completely. The only solution of this problem is to make mankind pure. Ignorance is the mother of all the evil and all the misery we see (C.W-I.p53).

'Remember that the nation lives in the cottage. But alas! Nobody raise them? Can you give them back their lost individuality without making them lose their innate spiritual nature? This is to be done and we will do it.'(C.W.V.p29)

"Forget not that the lower classes, the ignorant, the poor, the illiterate, the cobbler and the sweeper, are thy flesh and blood, thy brothers. Thou brave one, be bold, take courage, be proud that thou art an Indian, and proudly proclaim—I am an Indian—every Indian is my brother." Say "The ignorant Indian, the poor and destitute Indian, the Brahmin Indian, the pariah Indian, is my brother" (C.W-IV-p480).)

Do not stand on a high pedestal and take five cents in your hand and say, "Here, my poor man;“ but be greatful that the poor man is there, so that by making a gift to him you are able to help yourself, it is not the receiver that is blessed, but it is the giver. Be thankful that you are allowed to exercise your power of benevolence and mercy in the world, and this become pure and perfect.(II.299).

First bread and then religion, we stuff them too much with religion, when the poor fellows have been starving. No dogmas will satisfy the craving of hunger. You may talk doctrines by the millions, you may have sects by the hundreds of millions, ay, but it is nothing until you have the heart to feel; feel for them as your *Veda* teaches you. Till you find they are parts of your own bodies, till you realise that you are they, the poor and the rich, the saint and the sinner are all parts of one infinite whole, which you call *Brahman* (C.W.III,432).

This life is short, the vanities of the world are transient, but they alone live who live for others, the rest are more dead than alive (Letters of Swami Vivekananda- III).

Where would you go to seek for God; are not all the poor, the miserable, the weak, God? Why not worship them first? Why go to dig a well on the shores of the Ganga? (L.S.V.I4I).

So long as the millions live in hunger and ignorance I hold every man a traitor who, pays not the least heed to them (LSV.I75).

'I consider that the great national sin is the neglect of the masses, and that is one of the causes of our downfall. No amount of politics would be of any avail until the masses in India are once more well educated, well fed, and well cared for (CW.V.152).'

Feel, my children, feel; feel for the poor, the ignorant, the downtrodden; feel till the heart stops and the brain reels and you think you will go mad; then pour the soul out at the feet of the Lord, and then will come power, help, and indomitable energy. Struggle, struggle was my motto for the last ten years. Be not afraid my children (C.W. IV. 367).

There are many things to be done, but means are wanting in this country. We have brains, but no hands, have the doctrines of *Vedanta*, but we have not the power to reduce it into practice. I too believe that India will awake again. If anyone could love with all his heart the people of the country—bereft of the grace of affluence, of blasted fortune, their discreation totally lost, downtrodden, ever-starved, quarrelsome, and envious. Then only India will awake. When hundreds of large-hearted men and women, giving up all desires of enjoying the luxuries of life, will long and exert themselves to their utmost for the well-being of the millions of their countrymen who are gradually sinking lower and lower in the vortex of destitution and ignorance (C.W.125-24).

The only service to be done for our lower classes is to give them education, to develop their lost individuality. Give them ideas-that is the only help they require, and then the rest must follow as the effect. Ours is to put the chemicals together, the crystallization comes in the law of nature. Now if the mountain does not come to Mohammed, Mohammed must go to the mountain, if the poor boy cannot come to education, education must go to him.(IV.362-63)

The national ideals of India are renunciation and service, intensify her in those channels, and the rest will take care of itself (C.W-V-p228).)

10

Conclusion

Swami Vivekananda was a revolutionary thinker and a pragmatic philosopher. His philosophy was mainly concerned with the humanistic aspect of the social and spiritual life. However, his philosophy was more social than religious. He often said startling things. In fact, he had once said before a lecture that he was going to throw a few bombs. We can get an idea of the explosive nature of some of his statements if we read part of a letter which he wrote to his fellow disciples in the fall of 1894. He wrote ‘if you want any good to come, just throw your ceremonials overboard and worship the living God, the Man God—every being that wears a human form—God in his universal as well as individual aspect. The universal aspect of God means this world, and worshipping it means serving it - this indeed is work, not indulging in ceremonials (CW.Vol.6 p.265).

Swami Vivekananda as we sea expected all of the monks of the Order to serve the living God, which they do. This idea which may seem familar to us was an entirely new direction for an order of monks in India, and it had its origin directly in an experience of Shri Ramakrishna. As per the interpretation of Swami Vivekananda we are to serve the man God, we are to see humanity as divine, so that part of our service becomes the recognition of the divinity in men and women.

In India Swami Vivekananda awakened the in minds of the educated people of the glories of the ancient spiritual heritage and aroused their conscience with regard to their duties to the poor and downtrodden. He raised social service to the level of a national ideal, and invested it with the sanctity of worship and the power of a spiritual discipline.

His famous idea of serving man as God, '*Siva jnana jiva seva*,' was the essence of his social philosophy. This may be corroborated with the dictum *Atmannam Mokshyartham Jagadhitaya eka*. It means liberation of the self and the welfare of the world. He converted ordinary mundane forms of social service into worship. This is only possible through renunciation and self sacrifice.

The concept of *Vedanta Atmabat sarbabhutesu;* to look upon all being as your own self must be adopted in the philosophy of social service. Vivekananda therefore, said he who serves *jiva*, serves God indeed. 'One cannot help anyone but can only serve. This is the true worship of the God. First of all the worship is the worship of the *Virat*—of those all around us. One must give his body, mind and speech to the welfare of the world."

Swami Vivekananda had mentioned in his speech '*Matru-debo Bhava,pitru-debo Bhava-* look upon your mother as God, look upon your father as God'-but I say, *Daridra-debo Bhava ,Murkha-debo Bhava*-The poor, the illiterate, the ignorant, the afflicted-let these be your God." Know that service to these alone is the highest religion." (C.W.VI.288)

His philosophy was that, the only God to worship is the human soul in the human body. If one can do it in his practical life then in this world there would be no hatred, jealousy, sorrows and sufferings. No more struggle and evil thought—everywhere there will be peace and harmony. Gods will live then upon this earth. The very earth will then become heaven—that is the first great gain.

Indian thought speaks of three types of work in the service of society, namely, physical help through the removal of physical wants, intellectual help through the gift of secular education and work efficiency; and spiritual help through imparting spiritual knowledge. It ranks the last as the highest in the scale of values.

This philosophy of work bequeathed by the Indian spiritual tradition has the power within it to spiritually equip modern man to meet the challenge of the modern age. It has received new accessions of strength in our time from spiritual teachers like Swami Vivekanenda, "whose life and teachings", in the words of Dr. S. Radhakrishnan, "have prepared us for the new age of freedom in which we live. His spirit is supreme, man is unique. There is nothing inevitable in this world, and we can ward off the worst dangers and worst disabilities of which we are faced. Only we should not lose hope. He gave us fortitude in suffering he gave us hope in distress, he gave us courage in despair."

Swami Vivekananda, who did service to the world, came out of his intense feeling for its miseries. He gave the mandate to spiritual aspirants; "Give back the divine consciousness to all the poor, the downtrodden, the oppressed, and the sick." (CW.VIII-p.229). All these distressed and miserable people are not seperate from us, he stated. He said, according to *Advaitism*, love every man as your own self and not as your brother as in Christianity. Brotherhood should be superseded by universal selfhood. (CW.VI.P-I22) Here, God is direct. He is to be worshipped, while serving the poor and the diseased. An aspirant views him as God.

In the same way, Swami Vivekananda also tried to convince spiritual seekers that God would accept their services only if done with humility and reverence, without any taint of selfish desire for name, fame etc. Introducing the phrase *'Daridradevo Bhava'* he wanted to motivate us to serve the poor as God. He did not thereby deify hunger or indirectly contribute to perpetuation of poverty. Instead of offering ritual worship or chanting hymns in praise of God, a hungry man should be appeased by offering him food. To succeed in this discipline one needs a heart to feel, a brain to imagine and a strong arm to do the work.

He said we must work through love only. Every act of love brings peace and blessedness as its reaction. And love, when freely given in service to others, makes us calm and unattached. Real love is self-giving. We must love to serve God and to allow divine love to do perfect work through us. To remain unattached to our actions, and allow God to serve through us, we must serve God in the spirit of unselfish action and surrender the fruits of our actions to Him.

We must be prepared to sacrifice everything to God, and the best method to sacrifice ourselves to God is through service.

"Service naturally implies some kind of sacrifice. When a hungry man comes to you, give him a share of your food; when a poor man comes to you, give him a share of your wealth, similarly, you have to sacrifice your time, pleasure, energy etc. for the service of those who are ill, ignorant or suffering. Look upon everyone as a temple of God. By serving man, you are worshipping the Lord. This is the great idea behind Swami Vivekananda's philosophy of work" (Swami Yatiswarananda, Meditation and Spiritual life, p377).

"The miseries of the world cannot be cured by physical help only. Until man's nature changes, these physical needs will always arise and miseries will always be felt, and no amount of physical help will cure them completely. The only solution of this problem is to make mankind pure. Ignorance is the mother of all the evil and all the misery we see. Let men have light, let them be pure and spiritually strong and educated, then alone will misery cease in the world, not before. We may convert every house in the country into a charity asylum, we may fill the land with hospitals, but the misery of man will still continue to exist, until man's character changes." (C.W.Vol.I.P.53)

Swami Vivekananda's view on service can best be summed up in his poem, 'The Living God! (C.W.VII.P I62)

He who is in you and outside you,
Who works through all hands,
Who walks on all feet,
Whose body are all ye
Him worship, and break all other idols !

He who is at once the high and low,
The sinner and the saint,
Both God and worm,
Him worship-visible, knowable, real, omnipresent,
Break all other idols!

In whom is neither past life
Nor future birth nor death,
In whom we always have been
And always shall be one
Him worship. Break all other idols!

Ye fools! who neglect the living
And His infinite reflections with which
the world is full,
While ye run after imaginary shadows,
That lead alone to fights and quarrels,
Him worship, the only visible.
Break all other idols!

Thus, Swami Vivekananda's doctrine (philosophy) of service serves as a well-spring of faith and hope, feeding the flames of dedicated service to man as God in countless hearts. It not only assures redemption of individuals but promises revolutionary social changes.

Service is to be Characterised by goodwill and selfless love for all. Selfless love is the light of divinity latent in every individual. It is manifest when we do good to others. Without expecting a reward in return. The attitude are bent of mind behind the work are important, not the actual work.

Bibliography

Aurobindo,S., The Life Divine, Shri Aurobindo Ashrama, Pondichery, 1965

Ashokananda, S., a Call to the Eternal, Advaita Ashrama, Calcutta, 1995

Abhedananda, S., Complete Works of Swami Abhedananda Vedanta Math, Calcutta, 1967

Budhananda, S., The Saving Challenge of Religion

Ramakrishna Math, Madras, 1980

Chetanananda, S., Vedanta: Voice of Freedom, Advaita

Ashrama, Calcutta, 1991

Dasgapta R.K.; (Ed) Swami Vivekananda-A Hundred Years Lokeswarananda, Since Chicago (A Commemorative Volume)

Swami.; Pub; Ramakrishna Math and Ramakrishna Mission, Math, Belur Math Calcutta, 1994

Lokeswarananda, S., Practical Spirituality, The Rasmakrishna

Mission Institute of Culture, Calcutta

Mohapatra, A.R., Philosophy of Religion, Sterling pub, 1990

Ranganathanada,S., Swami Vivekananda; His Humanism,

Advaita Ashrama, Calcutta, 1996

Do Indian Philosophy of Social Work, Calcutta, 1967

Sivaramakrishna,M, (Ed.) Ramakrishna Vivekananda Vedanta Tradition, Sterling Publishers Pvt. Ltd 1991

Sharma, G.R., The Idealistic Philosophy of Swami Vivekananda,

Atlantic Publishers, New Delhi, 1987

Sharma, A, Ramakrishna and Vivekananda, Sterling Publishers Pvt. Ltd, New Delhi, 1989

Vivekananda, Swami., The Complete works of Swami Vivekananda

Advaita Ashrama, Calcutta, Vol-I-vIII. 1989

-do- My India the Eternal India. The Mission Institute of Culture, Calcutta, 1993.

-do- Pearls of Wisdom, The Ramakrishna Mission Institute of Culture, Calcutta, 1988

-do- Swamii Vivekananda on Universal Ethics and Moral Conduct, Ramakrishna Math, Hyderabad, 1974

-do- Vivekananda Speaks to You, Shri Ramakrishna Math, Madras, 1993

-do- Vivekananda: Man and His Message, Advaita Ashrama, Calcutta,

-do- Vivekananda; The Great Spiritual Teacher, Advaita Ashrama, Calcutta, 1995

Vivekananda, S., Teaching of Swami Vivekananda,sa, .Advaita Ashrama, Calcutta

-do- Reminiscences of Swami Vivekananda, Advaita Ashrama, Calcutta

-do- Talks with Swami Vivekananda, Advaita Ashrama, Calcutta

-do- Rebuild India Ramakrishna Math, Belur, Calcutta, 1989.

-do- Proletariat Win Equal Rights, Advaita Ashrama, Calcutta, 1984

-do- Vivekananda His Call to the Nation- Advaita Ashrama, Calcutta,1969

-do- Caste, Culture and Socialism, Advaita Ashrama Calcutta

-do- Vivekananda and His Humanism, Advaita Ashrama, Calcutta

do- Vivekananda and his Human Excellence, Advaita Ashrama, Calcutta

-do- State, Society and Socialism, Adavaita Ashrama Calcutta

-do- Service and Spirituality, Madras Math, Madras

Vamanananda, S, Eternal platform, Ramakrishna Ashrama, Ramharipur, 1993 (Pub)

Yetiswarananda, S., Meditation and Spiritual Life, Sri Ramakrishna Ashrama, Bangalore, 1979

Index